PRAISE FOR BE FEARLESS

"OUTSTANDING! Julie Clinton's devotional, *Be Fearless,* is the perfect start to each day. The practical applications illustrated in the pages of this book make God's word come alive. The quotes from famous teachers and contemporary faith heroes, along with the sprinkling of amazing words from worship songs, bring a richness that artfully waters the soul."

Shelene Bryan,
bestselling author of *Love, Skip, Jump*
and *Ridiculous Faith*

"There is nothing I love more than spending time meditating on God's word. However, life's crazy schedules sometimes make setting aside time seem impossible. Julie has given us a brilliantly crafted, bite-sized collection of thoughts to tackle a big topic: FEAR. Using time-tested truths in God's word, she inspires and instructs us to live fearlessly by reminding us that God is faithful. In ninety days of meditating on God's word, you can go from worrier to warrior."

Bianca Juarez Olthoff,
teacher, preacher, church planter,
author of the bestselling book, *Play with Fire*

"Do you ever wish you could have a good friend sit down with you every day and remind you that God loves you right now, just as you are? That's what my friend Julie does in the beautiful book. She reminds us that we can live a fearless life and shows us how. What a gift."

Sheila Walsh,
author of *In the Middle of the Mess*

"Reading Julie Clinton's words is like sitting across the table from a trustworthy friend and mentor who gets you and loves you too much to let you settle for less than God's best in your life! In *Be Fearless,* Julie shows us how to overcome our greatest fears with Biblical truths forged into daily decisions that establish our courage as a woman God created for a purpose! Packed with real-life application and powerful truths, *Be Fearless* is a message every woman needs. Grab a copy for yourself and a friend!"

Renee Swope,
bestselling author of *A Confident Heart*

"Over the past few years I have had the pleasure of working along-side Julie in ministry, and it's an honor to recommend her devotional, *Be Fearless*. She is a true woman of God on and off the stage, and time and time again she has impressed me with her love for Christ and heart for women. I have already started this devotional and it has been wonderful. I know you'll love it as much as I do!"

Angie Smith,
national women's ministry speaker,
bestselling author of multiple books,
including *Seamless: Understanding
the Bible as One Complete Story*

BE FEARLESS

Published by Forefront Books.

Cover Design by Bruce Gore, Gore Studio Inc.
Interior Design by Bill Kersey, KerseyGraphics

ISBN: 978-1-948-67710-3
ISBN: 978-1-948-67711-0 (eBook)

BE FEARLESS

An Extraordinary Women
90 Day Devotional

JULIE CLINTON
with DINA JONES

ACKNOWLEDGMENTS

*First and foremost, I would like to thank my heavenly Father for the lessons, bless-*ings, friendships, and experiences that have been woven into these pages. May this book be only to your glory.

Thank you to my loving husband, Tim. I love our lives together and your commitment to impacting the world for Christ.

Megan, you are a brilliant and fearless Proverbs 31 woman. Your dad and I couldn't be more proud of you or love you more. Thank you for setting such an example for so many—of loving service to the Lord, kindness in all that you do, and tireless compassion for all you encounter.

Zach, thank you for the joy and laughter you bring to my life. Your dad and I love watching you use your talents for the Lord and be a trusted friend to so many.

Thank you, Ben, for loving our daughter and being a wonderful son-in-law.

Dina, your writing assistance has been deeply impactful to this project. Thank you for your passion and dedication to bringing *Be Fearless* to life. We can't wait to see what the Lord continues to do with your talent.

Amy, Beth, Jenny, Angela, Kim, and the entire Extraordinary Women team: your friendship, prayers, and service to Extraordinary

Women Ministries are more appreciated and valuable than you know. Thank you for all the things you do, especially the diligent behind-the-scenes commitment to our EW community. You are loved and valued beyond what you can ever imagine, and I am blessed to serve with you!

Special thanks to Lindsay and Emily for your creativity, hard work, and reverent handling of Scripture. Working with you is a delight and encouragement.

Pat, thank you for lending your wisdom to this project. You are a blessing to our ministry and we remain grateful for our friendship and work with you.

Kyle, thank you for organizing meetings, logistics, and details with such a fun and hardworking attitude. You keep us all smiling.

Patty, thank you for hearing my heart and working tirelessly to help find the best words for the message.

To the Extraordinary Women Community: your passion and enthusiasm for growing in your relationships with the Lord is so refreshing and inspiring; it makes our work rewarding.

TABLE OF CONTENTS

INTRODUCTION

In our broken world, we are often confronted with scary, painful situations that take a toll on us physically, mentally, emotionally, and even spiritually. As women, we also tend to carry concern for the people we care most about. If we are not careful to effectively process our feelings and emotions, then watching our children, parents, spouses, and friends face cancer, divorce, job loss, and other devastations can leave us fearful and uncertain.

Recently, the #MeToo movement has focused a lot of attention on the stories of women who have suffered intimidation, harassment, and abuse—much of it sexual. Every day, previously hidden stories are being brought out of the darkness and into the light. I am deeply saddened to think of the talent, creativity, and potential that have been squelched in so many promising women by the evil forces arrayed against them.

In many ways, the #MeToo movement is simply the unfolding of an ongoing story of bias and discrimination against women, a story in which, sadly, the church has often played the wrong role. Our Savior's model for dealing with women is completely different. Jesus treated women with respect, love, and care, empowering them to live lives free from intimidation and shame.

Consider these biblical examples.

Rahab was a heathen harlot, but God used her to protect an entire nation, and then blessed her whole family! Ruth was a grieving widow who had no relationship with the one true God, but He redeemed her, gave her a godly husband, and through her descendants brought His son Jesus into the world! And when Jesus spoke the truth in love to a promiscuous woman at a well, her life was changed, and she brought the whole city to Him!

Scripture constantly reminds us not to allow ourselves to be overwhelmed by fear and anxiety. Living fearlessly is really about being a woman who has found her way with God and has experienced his faithfulness to her, even—and especially—in the dark. When you live as a fearless woman, you know that He's your Abba Father, that He's seeing you through, that He's carrying you, and that He'll never leave you or forsake you.

But is it hard? Absolutely.

The great challenge? Living well in this big, old, fallen world.

Yet despite the darkness around us—and the brokenness within us—we really can become free. We really can run fearlessly forward in this world with the femininity and strength that exemplify life-changing beauty.

That's my dream for you as you encounter the truth on each page of this devotional; that you will move to a place where you chase dreams and live beyond the anxiety of everyday life ... fearlessly.

Julie

FRESH AND NEW

*"Because of the Lord's great love we are not consumed,
for his compassions never fail. They are new every
morning; great is your faithfulness. I say to myself, "The
Lord is my portion; therefore I will wait for him."*
~ LAMENTATIONS 3:22–24 (NIV)

Daily Meditation: Philippians 2, 2 Corinthians 5:11–21

The dew on the ground, the small green blades of grass poking out of the lawn after a hard winter, the warmth of the sun's rays on a cold morning, they all shout "fresh and new" to me. It's a new day!

God's faithfulness is like that. Even after a hard season, a broken heart, or a long battle, His faithfulness never runs out, and His compassions never fail. They are new every morning. Every moment of every day, love and compassion are fresh and new from our heavenly Father. He doesn't run out of anything. He always has plenty of whatever we need.

Indeed, "The Lord is my portion," for He is more than everything we need. He is always much more than enough for us. In that we can rejoice!

As women, we may run out of energy, strength, passion, or patience. We might feel like we are "at the end of our rope" or just "so done" with the day's challenges. It is at these junctures that we must stop and make sure we are staying connected to the Lord so that He can renew our strength. The Lord wants to pour new mercies onto and into us, but He will not force himself on us; we must seek Him. When we are feeling exhausted and overwhelmed, we can buy into the lie that we don't have time for relationship with the Lord, but the exact opposite is true. It is only with the Lord's strength that we can continue living well. We can do all things—persist in all situations, hold fast to our faith no matter the circumstances—"through Christ who strengthens" us (Philippians 4:13).

> *"Sanctification, again, is the outcome and inseparable*
> *consequence of regeneration. He who is born again*
> *and made a new creature, receives a new nature and*
> *a new principle and always lives a new life."*
> -J. C. RYLE

———————

BE FEARLESS: *thankfully, the fact that we can run out of gas, run ourselves ragged, or even run on empty is in no way a reflection of our Father! He never runs out. And yes, we can reflect Him by giving to others, but only when we are anchored in Him. So renew yourself each morning by plugging into the only unlimited source of life, power, and peace.*

LIVING FEARLESSLY

"There is no fear in love. But perfect love drives out fear ..."
~ 1 JOHN 4:18 (NIV)

Daily Meditation: Isaiah 35:4, 2 Timothy 1:7

One of the hallmarks of a healthy relationship is safety. Without a feeling of safety, you can't fully place your trust in a person, because there's always a fear that they will betray it. If you feel unsafe, can you really trust that person with your heart? And when you don't have a sense of security, you can often feel overwhelmed or be driven by fear. We may even experience this fear with God.

Fears have a way of seeping into our minds, blowing in like unseen drafts of air on a cold wintery morning: we don't know where they come from, but we can feel the chill. In my ongoing search for wisdom and growth, I have reread that verse about "perfect love drives out fear" again and again and again. I have heard it a hundred times, but every time I read it I feel a warm breeze blowing on my soul, a comforting presence in my heart. Jesus is the embodiment of perfect love; He casts out my fear!

How sure am I that my Father in heaven loves me? Well, when I am fully confident of His love for me, right at that precise moment fear fades. It is as if the fireplace in my soul turns on. You know the warmth I'm talking about. You've felt it before. It goes way beyond your cold feet, all the way down into the inner reaches of your soul, and it feels so good. That is our Father! To walk freely, boldly, and fearlessly is to be a daughter holding her Father's hand.

> *"Fear lurks in the shadows of every area of life. The future may look very threatening. Jesus says, "Stop being afraid. Trust me!"*
> ~ CHARLES SWINDOLL

BE FEARLESS: *fears always seem to come with claws that grip us and hold us tight. That sensation is not of God! His love can "declaw" our fears and living fearlessly is the result. Now go, and may you forever feel His warm breath upon you.*

DO NOT FEAR

"So do not fear, for I am with you;
do not be dismayed, for I am your God.
I will strengthen you and help you; I will uphold
you with my righteous right hand."
~ ISAIAH 41:10 (NIV)

Daily Meditation: Isaiah 41, 1 John 4

When I was little, my bedroom was on the other side of the house from my parents.
The cellar and garage doors were between us. At night, a creaking floorboard or a gust of wind through the billowing trees outside my window could seem unsettling and scary. As a child, the few feet between my parents' bedroom and my little bed could seem like several miles—and it was dark. The fear that seeped in would cause me to forget that I was safe.

As grown women, our fears are different. We may no longer be afraid of the dark, but perhaps a family member's diagnosis, a flailing relationship, an adult child turning away from their faith, or a pervasive sense of loneliness is causing us to tremble.

Fear is a powerful emotion. It can intimidate or cripple us. As a result, we may become defensive and timid. Fear can immobilize us or even make us physically ill. And just like my childhood fear kept me from remembering that my parents were close and I was safe, our adult fears can make us forget that we are our safe in our heavenly Father's arms, especially in the dark. Psalm 56:3–4 (NIV) states, "When I am afraid, I put my trust in you. In God, whose word I praise—in God I trust and am not afraid . . . ."

From the beginning of time, God has reminded His people to not be afraid. Though fear may seem to be embedded in our nature, we must boldly remind ourselves of who we are in Christ. Galatians 4:7 (NIV) states, "So you are no longer a slave, but God's child; and since you are his child, God has made you also an heir." God desires a relationship with us. We are known by Him. He loves us, and He is for us. The reassuring phrases "Fear not" and "Be not afraid" are used in the Bible over a hundred times.

You don't have to be afraid of anything, and that includes darkness, death or life, angels or demons, the present or the future, or any powers in all of creation, because nothing can ever separate you from God's love (Romans 8:38–39).

> *"Feed your fears and your faith will starve.*
> *Feed your faith and your fears will starve."*
> ~MAX LUCADO

BE FEARLESS: *the fact that we are free not to fear is liberating! It brings true peace and rest, and it even promotes sweet sleep. The Lord covers us, shields us, and watches over us. Freed from fear, we can rest—and even run and dance—in our freedom.*

GO AHEAD, CALL THEIR CARDS

"But Jesus said to them, 'I have shown you many good works
from the Father. For which of these do you stone me?'"
~ JOHN 10:32 (NIV)

Daily Meditation: John 10, Matthew 18:15–22

There is a time and a place for everything, and sometimes it's time to stand up for the
truth! That's when I draw a line in the sand, the point where I
simply must stand up and tell it like it is. My kids and husband
know that point well.

I'm sure you've been there too. While I do make it my goal to
"speak the truth in love" (Ephesians 4:15), I also admire how Jesus
stood up to his attackers (they wanted to stone him) and said, "I
have shown you many good works . . . for which of these do you
stone me?"

He called their cards. He did so in love, but He didn't shy away
from the conflict. This was a defining moment, and he was going
to make them choose, based on fact, what they were going to do.
He didn't stand by and ignore the fact that they were wrong: He
confronted them with the truth in a righteous and loving manner.

You and I probably aren't about to be stoned, but other kinds of attacks are common in our day. We may be victims of bullying, blackmail, backstabbing, gossiping, and even violence, but there is a time and a place to call their cards. When it's your time, tell it like it is! Don't be afraid. You are in charge. Tell the truth. Speak up for what is right, whether for you or for others.

> *"Stand before the people you fear and speak*
> *your mind—even if your voice shakes."*
> ~Maggie Kuhn

———————

BE FEARLESS: *calling someone's cards is not an everyday event. It's hard to do because you need to be prayerful and listen for God's direction. And it can be intimidating! But you owe it to others, yourself, and the person who is wrong to let the truth ring out.*

IMITATION, NOT PERFECTION

"Follow God's example, therefore, as dearly loved children."
~ EPHESIANS 5:1 (NIV)

Daily Meditation: Ephesians 4:17–32, Ephesians 5:1–20

Think of a child you dearly love. Perhaps you have your own children, or maybe there is a special niece, nephew, or student in your life. No matter how adorable, precious, and cherished the child is, that special someone is far from perfect. Do you expect perfection from him or her? How would you feel if you learned that the child you love was waiting to achieve perfection or at least get a bit closer to perfection before spending more time in relationship with you?

In the fourth and fifth chapters of Ephesians, we read a number of expectations for our walk as Christians. Our words are to be edifying, our hearts grateful, and our time fruitful. Yet we do not need to achieve perfection in these areas in order for us to have a close relationship with the Lord.

Instead, as dearly loved children, we are called to imitate the God who created us. Children are imitators, but although we are privileged to be children of the one true source of goodness, we simply cannot become truly "good" on our own. So instead of getting caught up in a cycle of trying to do better, become more holy, and be more perfect, let's stop and focus on childlike imitation. To imitate someone, we must pay close attention to who they are and what they do. We can imitate the Lord only when we are paying attention to what He is like.

Let us adopt this mindset now—not at some point in the future, but on this very day. How can we imitate Jesus *today*? What if right now we stepped back from all the standards we measure ourselves by and instead fixed our eyes on Jesus? What if we trusted Him to hold us and guide us as we seek to imitate His love in our daily lives?

We really can "walk in love" (Ephesians 5:2a) and not in fear. Today let us forget our earthly ideas of perfection, whether motivated by pride, anxiety, or insecurity. Instead, let us imitate our Father as cherished children. Let us take shelter in our nearness to Him.

> "In your nearness I take shelter. Where you are is where I'm home.
> I have need of only one thing: To be here before your throne."
> ~MEREDITH ANDREWS, "DRAW ME NEARER"

BE FEARLESS: *trust the Lord in this: if you keep your eyes on Him, He will guide you in becoming more like him. Spend time worshiping the Lord and reading His word instead of mentally running through your own expectations and desires of perfection.*

A LONGING FULFILLED

*"Hope deferred makes the heart sick, but a
longing fulfilled is a tree of life."*
~ PROVERBS 13:12 (NIV)

Daily Meditation: Isaiah 54, Isaiah 55

Have you ever deeply longed for something that felt out of reach? It can be hard to have hope when the bills go unpaid, the kids are out of control, or you don't feel cared for, loved, or appreciated. Maybe it's hard for you to imagine why the Lord wouldn't grant your plea for a certain deep longing. Your desires may be perfectly godly, like meeting a Christ-honoring soul mate, becoming pregnant with your first child, or being granted a clean bill of health. These yearnings, as well as others like becoming debt-free or seeing an errant child come back home, are all honest desires, and it can be hard to wait for them to take place. Perhaps you have become deeply discouraged at the distance between where you are today and where you want to be.

I've learned time and time again over the years that the creator of life is not finished with us, even if our hope starts to run thin. Think of your life as a garden or a forest. The Lord may be planting seeds below the surface that you cannot see, and you don't have to have a green thumb to know that beautiful plants and trees do not appear overnight.

Remember that in His omniscient power, God knows far more than we do about what we need and when we need it. Isaiah 55:8–9 (NKJV) provides a powerful reminder: "For My thoughts are not your thoughts, Nor are your ways My ways," says the Lord. "For as the heavens are higher than the earth, So are My ways higher than your ways, And My thoughts than your thoughts."

In time, as I press forward and look to Him, I witness a tender green shoot coming out of a seemingly dead situation. Then another, and before I know it, the burnt remains of my ideal forest are looking lush and green! Time after time, my Father in heaven finds a way to turn my longings into "a tree of life!" Next time your heart is aching, imagine the Lord planting seeds in your garden and let hope wash over you.

> *"The most difficult time in your life may be*
> *the border to your promised land."*
> ~ CHRISTINE CAINE

———————

BE FEARLESS: *the Lord is not required to fulfill all our wishes, but He does make promises to us. John Piper says, "Christian hope is when God has promised that something is going to happen and you put your trust in that promise. Christian hope is a confidence that something will come to pass because God has promised it will come to pass." God has promised to direct our paths (Proverbs 3:5–6), give us rest (Matthew 11:28), and be with us in our trials (Isaiah 43:2), among thousands of additional promises found in his word. Our hope is in God.*

TRADE UP!

"... to bestow on them a crown of beauty instead of ashes,
the oil of joy instead of mourning,
and a garment of praise instead of a spirit of despair."
~ ISAIAH 61:3A (NIV)

Daily Meditation: Isaiah 61, Isaiah 62

HGTV's Fixer Upper *with Chip and Joanna Gaines built quite a following.* I absolutely love to watch Chip and Joanna trade out some outdated or dilapidated "features" of a home for beautiful new designs. A rotting stairway is traded up for a beautiful new craftsman staircase. Two small, dark rooms are traded up for one large and gorgeous space with new lighting.

Our lives can seem like "fixer upper" situations too, with endless trades made by the Lord. God loves to "trade up" in my life. Here are just a few of the improvements He has promised to make:

- To take my ashes and give me a "crown of beauty"
- To swap my mourning for the "oil of joy"
- To exchange my spirit of despair for a "garment of praise"

Sometimes I'm not sure why the Lord chooses to do His work in *me.* Just like those houses Chip and Joanna scope out, I find myself an unlikely vessel. Yet the Lord pours His kindness on me, continually and freely exchanging His blessings for my burdens. It may take some work and some surrender, but each of us can become new in Him.

> "Let God speak in your life. Let his father heart come
> and say, 'this is what I have for you'
> …fixing our eyes on Jesus and walking in that truth."
> ~ JOANNA GAINES

BE FEARLESS: *what can you surrender to the Lord today? Do you have bitterness, worry, or another burden that you can allow Him to take from you?*

YOU ARE LOVED

"The Lord your God in your midst, the Mighty One, will save;
He will rejoice over you with gladness, He will quiet you with
His love,
He will rejoice over you with singing."
~ ZEPHANIAH 3:17 (NKJV)

Daily Meditation: Galatians 2:20, 1 John 3

Over the years, I have counseled many women who have a blind spot when it comes to God's love. Oh, they believe that God *is* love, that He loves the world and the sinner and their neighbor. Yet it is difficult for them to let the reality sink in that God loves them—personally. God really loves *you*. Deeply, passionately, individually—God loves *you*.

There are several factors that contribute to a woman's difficulty in understanding and accepting that she is loved. Perhaps it is a painful past or deep insecurity. There may be an old sin or unfulfilled longing. Once a seed of doubt is sown ("Does God really love *me?*"), we can allow circumstances and fears to push us further down the path of disbelief in God's love for us.

Part of what makes it so sad to see women doubting God's love for them is the sheer magnitude of His love. Scripture tells us that not only does God love us, He delights in us. I love that thought and image of my Father in heaven delighting in me. He is not just tolerating or putting up with me!

Although we may feel unloved, that is simply untrue. The truth is that you are the object of His affection day in and day out. He wants you, He likes you, He pursues you, and He enjoys being with you. The state of your house, car, hair, bank account, or laundry in no way affects His love for you. The same holds true for husbands, children, jobs, or lack thereof. Nothing in this world can hinder, not even in the slightest, His great love for you and me.

> *"It's not about finding ways to avoid God's judgment*
> *and feeling like a failure if you don't do everything perfectly.*
> *It's about fully experiencing God's love and letting it perfect you.*
> *It's not about being somebody you are not.*
> *It's about becoming who you really are."*
> ~ STORMIE OMARTIAN

BE FEARLESS: *how would your life look if you truly believed that God wants you, likes you, and loves you? How would you feel when you wake up in the morning, when you go to bed at night, when there are trying circumstances, and when you are alone?*

TO THE FUTURE

> *"For I know the plans I have for you," declares the Lord,*
> *"plans to prosper you and not to harm you, plans*
> *to give you hope and a future."*
> ~ JEREMIAH 29:11 (NIV)

Daily Meditation: Psalm 107, Psalm 108

Life seems to have a way of throwing us curveballs, sometimes at what feels like the absolute worst moment. Sometimes these curveballs are minor annoyances or events that become funny with time, but at other times there is nothing minor or humorous about what comes our way. The death of a loved one. A car crash. A cancer diagnosis. Deep disappointment.

When our world gets rocked, it can be hard to hope for the future. It's easy to get angry, resentful, or even bitter—anxious about what happens next.

Proverbs 31 describes the worthy woman in verse 25 as being able to (depending on the translation) "laugh" or "smile" at the future, as she is clothed in strength and dignity. How can we put on a cloak of strength and smile at the future?

We can start by reminding ourselves of God's goodness, omniscience, and love for us.

- God is good. Psalm 106:1 reminds us to praise the Lord for His goodness. He alone is good.
- Good is omniscient. God is all-knowing. While we may not understand a current or past trial, the Lord sees all. He knows how to work any situation for our good.
- God loves us. God is love, and his love for us is expressed over and over in scripture. God expresses His love in many ways, but the epitome of His love for us is shown in sending His only son to die for us.
- God is our father. His love for us is the protective and tender love of a perfect parent.

"I'm never alone
You're a good, good father
It's who you are, it's who you are, it's who you are
And I'm loved by you"
~ CHRIS TOMLIN "GOOD GOOD FATHER"

BE FEARLESS: *He will … He IS … seeing you through. Hold on!*

GOOD IN ALL THINGS

*"We can rejoice, too, when we run into problems and trials, for
we know that they help us develop endurance. And endurance
develops strength of character, and character strengthens
our confident hope of salvation. And this
hope will not lead to disappointment."*

~ ROMANS 5:3–5A (NLT)

Daily Meditation: Psalm 31, Mark 10:17–31

Rejoice when we run into problems and trials? Are you kidding me? How can pain, the frantic pace of my day, and all kinds of pressure produce anything good in my life? "It gets old!" That's how I feel at times.

But there is good in it somewhere; there always is, for "endurance develops strength of character," and we all want that. Even if the situation seems utterly impossible, we can cling to the fact that "this hope will not lead to disappointment." I like that! I'm learning to stay quiet and hold on . . . and to rejoice more and more in the journey. Even though some seasons are indeed hurtful, lengthy, and maybe even off-the-charts crazy, it's during those same seasons that the fruit of character is being produced in me, fruit that I'll get to enjoy for days to come. It's always darkest before the light.

I have cried tears of deep pain, tears that seemed to burn up before they hit the ground. At times I have felt desperate, believed the situation was unjust, and been thoroughly convinced that there was no chance for any good to come from the pain. So I thought, but good did come. It always does. Remember: "This too shall pass."

> *"When a train goes through a tunnel and it gets dark,*
> *you don't throw away the ticket and jump*
> *off. You sit still and trust the engineer."*
> ~ CORRIE TEN BOOM

BE FEARLESS: *our heavenly Father will always be there, holding our hands, never letting go, and always caring about our holiness before our happiness. Take that next step forward. Good is coming!*

GRACE IS YOURS

"But God demonstrates his own love for us in this:
While we were still sinners, Christ died for us."
~ ROMANS 5:8 (NIV)

Daily Meditation: I Peter 5, Titus 2:11–15

Is there anything as amazing as the grace of the Lord?

Today's verse, Romans 5:8, does not read, "While we tried really hard, Christ died for us," or "When we gave up our habitual sin and prayed and fasted, God gave us grace." No. God's love for us is demonstrated "while we were still sinners," and no matter how spiritually mature we become, we never grow beyond our need for God's grace.

We can never be good enough to earn God's love, acceptance, and forgiveness. His grace is the only way for us to have a relationship with Him. We are given *sufficient grace* to persevere through trials (2 Corinthians 12:8–9). Grace is given in *various forms* through our gifts (I Peter 4:10). When we are humble, God gives us *more grace* (James 4:6). Grace is given to us in *abundance* (2 Peter 1:2).

Sometimes we operate as if God's grace were scarce. Can I really come to God with yet another request for forgiveness? Will God hear my prayer in spite of all my past failures? Can I walk in peace and confidence, free from shame or insecurity, knowing that God's grace has covered me? The answer is always "yes."

Sufficient Grace. Abundant Grace. Amazing Grace.

> *"Amazing Grace, how sweet the sound that saved a wretch like me.*
> *I once was lost but now am found, was blind but now I see."*
> ~ JOHN NEWTON

BE FEARLESS: *sometimes our fear, insecurity, or shame can hinder us from fully feeling and receiving the grace of God. Meditate today on one of the scriptures from our devotion: 2 Corinthians 12:8–9, 1 Peter 4:10, James 4:6, or 2 Peter 1:2. Thank God for His grace right now. As you walk through your day today, keep in mind that you are walking through life covered in God's free and unmerited love and blessings, His grace.*

DESIRING WISDOM

*"If any of you lacks wisdom, you should ask God,
who gives generously to all without finding
fault, and it will be given to you."*
~ JAMES 1:5 (NIV)

Daily Meditation: James 1, James 2, James 3:13–18

Give me a heart of wisdom ... that's what Solomon asked for. He didn't ask for more time or money, although he could have asked for anything at all. Instead of wealth, fame, or fortune, he chose wisdom, and God blessed him with everything imaginable.

What do you want more than anything? What do you dream about and long for? For many women, the honest answer would be a romantic relationship, physical beauty, finances, a child, or maybe simply some rest. Sometimes a difficult or confusing circumstance can shift that perspective, and with sudden clarity we realize what we really need: Faith. Strength. *Wisdom*. Wisdom is not mere knowledge, but knowledge applied.

God says that He gives us wisdom "without finding fault." There is no guilt or shame in asking God for wisdom or help. He does not require—much less expect—us to have all the answers. Even if we are in a situation caused by our own wrongdoing, the Lord will grant us wisdom. He wants us to simply ask Him, and He gives it "generously"!

> *"Wisdom is the right use of knowledge. To know is not to be wise.*
> *Many men know a great deal, and are all the greater fools for it.*
> *There is no fool so great a fool as a knowing fool.*
> *But to know how to use knowledge is to have wisdom."*
> ~ CHARLES SPURGEON

———————

BE FEARLESS: *is there an area of your life in which you feel uncertain? Is there an area where you feel stuck or unsure? Pray right now for wisdom in that area. Know that your prayers are heard. God never lets us down.*

SEASONS

"There is a time for everything, and a season
for every activity under the heavens:"
~ ECCLESIASTES 3:1 (NIV)

Daily Meditation: Ecclesiastes 3, Ecclesiastes 4, Daniel 2:17–23

Thousands of years had gone by from the creation of the world until Jesus walked the earth. He waited until He was thirty to begin His ministry, and then it only lasted three short years. We know that Father God was not waiting for Jesus to develop better character, so He must have had a plan and a purpose in His timing of every last detail. Although I may not always understand it, there certainly is "a time for every- thing." I don't know every season that is coming, but I do know I can trust that God is aware of me, my needs, and my desires. I can rest in Him.

Sometimes it's easier for us to appreciate the seasons of the past or the future than it is for us to embrace our current season. We do not know why we have to prepare so long, or if our dream will ever come to fruition. We may look to the past or the future with rose-colored glasses yet feel the full stress of today. There is a reason for the season you are in, sister. Do not wish it away. There are gifts available to you now that you may not fully recognize until weeks, months, or even years from today.

I may not understand it, but I can know without a doubt that there is "a time for everything." I don't know every season that is coming, but I know I can trust that God meets me right where I am. Right now. Right here. Chose to blossom where you are planted. Let Him lead you into your tomorrow.

"Even when it hurts
Even when it's hard
Even when it all just falls apart
I will run to You
'Cause I know that You are
Lover of my soul
Healer of my scars
You steady my heart"
~ KARI JOBE

BE FEARLESS: *challenge yourself to spend some time this week specifically thanking God for your current season. Write down several very short-term goals for making the most out of today and this week.*

IT ALL MATTERS

*"Jesus answered him, 'What I am doing you do not understand now,
but afterward you will understand.'"*
~ JOHN 13:7 (ESV)

Daily Meditation: Habakkuk 2:3, Psalm 46

Women are often dreamers. God often plants a deep desire in our heart to bring meaning and beauty to situations and environments around us, but sometimes the sheer weight of our "regular" daily demands can be crushing. Does your to-do list ever look like this?

- Tackle the seemingly endless mountain of laundry
- Prepare meals and snacks for yourself and/or for others
- Take everyone where they need to go
- Clean
- Exercise
- Make that doctor's appointment
- Check on and/or care for your aging parents
- Maintain friendships or a romantic relationship
- Stay on top of various duties at work

Interestingly, many of the things that we see as highly inefficient "time wasters" are actually part of God's process. The responsibilities that come with our roles and seasons of life cultivate character. The word "work" is mentioned over 400 times in the Bible!

When I am tempted to become weary in my responsibilities, I am reminded of *Practicing the Presence of God* by Brother Lawrence, a monk whose primary job in the monastery was to scrub pots for years. He found his menial task was actually a holy opportunity to commune with God. As he scrubbed and cleaned, Brother Lawrence put together one of the most widely read books on developing an awareness of the presence of God. Perhaps we can fold our laundry, scrub our pots, or exercise as an act of worship, intentionally focusing our thoughts on being aware of God's presence.

Instead of railing against our seemingly boring responsibilities, let's look for the blessings in them. Work on cultivating your character in the little tasks and challenges along the way. Like Janet Stuart, strive to graciously accept interruptions or setbacks, and when God does bring along a new opportunity, you will have built a solid foundation for it.

> *"She delighted in seeing her plan upset by unexpected events, saying*
> *that it gave her great comfort, and that she looked on such things*
> *as an assurance that God was watching over her stewardship*
> *. . . she was joyfully and graciously ready to recognize the indication*
> *of God's ruling hand, and to allow herself to be guided by it."*
> ~ FROM *The Life and Letters of Janet Erskine Stuart*

BE FEARLESS: *it is not our job to huff and puff at God when He does things His way according to His schedule. It is our job as stewards to use our time wisely and be faithful in our responsibilities.*

TAKE MY HAND

*"For I am the LORD your God who takes
hold of your right hand and says to you,
Do not fear; I will help you."*
~ ISAIAH 41:13 (NIV)

Daily Meditation: Psalm 144:7–8, Ephesians 4

When my children, Megan and Zach, were little and we were either crossing the
street or just working our way back to our car in the parking lot, I
would grab their hands. It was natural. I wanted to keep them safe.
I wanted to guide them. I wanted to hold them close so I could
direct them quickly if need be.

Reading that God "takes hold of your right hand" is the exact same
thing. I don't have to walk alone! I can close my eyes and see my heavenly Father grabbing my hand before we even step off the first curb. He
is right there with me to guide me through life's unknown situations.
And as much as I love to do that with my own children, how much
more does God love to do that with His children—with you and me!
There is something so profoundly reassuring for us in the simple act
of holding hands! He actually *wants* to take my hand. And then He so
lovingly adds, "Do not fear; I will help you."

Go on; hold His hand tightly. Don't try to walk this earth alone. On our own we can so easily get lost or trampled down by the chaos coming our way. But when we cling to God's hand and let Him guide us through the crazy obstacles of life, we know that He is with us no matter what!

> *"Neither go back in fear and misgiving to the past, nor*
> *in anxiety and forecasting to the future; but lie*
> *quiet under His hand, having no will but His."*
> ~ H. E. MANNING

BE FEARLESS: *holding hands—whether with a date, spouse, child, or grandchild—has to rank right up there with some of the most precious experiences we enjoy in this life! Thankfully, we can repeat the action of holding hands a million times over. Do it today and remember that your Father has His hand in yours.*

LOVE IN DISCIPLINE

*"During the forty years that I led you through the wilderness,
your clothes did not wear out, nor did the sandals on your feet."*
~ DEUTERONOMY 29:5 (NIV)

Daily Meditation: Deuteronomy 29, Proverbs 19

Most parents don't want to be seen as heavy disciplinarians. Yet, as a parent, there were times when I had to discipline my children not because I no longer loved them, but because I loved them so much. No doubt you remember the story of the children of Israel. For forty years they wandered in the desert. Had God abandoned them? No. God never left them, not even in the midst of their disobedience and rebellion. Look at His blanket of love over the situation:

- God was displeased with them, yet He fed them.
- He was angry with them, yet He clothed them.
- He wanted to destroy them, yet He kept their sandals from wearing out.
- They were in the wrong, yet He gave them water to drink.
- They sinned, yet He stayed with them.

Love and discipline go together like chocolate and peanut butter, but we often see them as oil and vinegar, two things that don't mix. The problem with our viewpoint occurs when we look at love and discipline from a human perspective. Although, sadly, some people do tend to withhold love when they are disciplining their children, that is not the case with God. He does the impossible even while He is disciplining us: His love for us never changes or falters, not even when He is disappointed in us and is applying His divine discipline to nudge us back to Him! That truth brings me such peace and appreciation, and it's one more reason why He is worthy of my trust and devotion!

> "God is interested in developing your
> character. At times He lets you proceed,
> but He will never let you go too far without
> discipline to bring you back.
> In your relationship with God, He may let you make a wrong
> decision. Then the Spirit of God causes you to recognize that
> it is not God's will. He guides you back to the right path."
> ~ HENRY BLACKABY

BE FEARLESS: *love is something we all want and need. Thankfully, God is our perfect model in all things love-related. He loves us perfectly 24/7, even when that love involves discipline! Know that His love never changes even in the middle of tough times, and even if you have caused the difficult situation you're in. Let that reality comfort your soul.*

RELATIONSHIPS ARE WORTH IT

"By this everyone will know that you are my
disciples, if you love one another."
~ JOHN 13:35 (NIV)

Daily Meditation: 1 Corinthians 13, Romans 12

At one time or another, we've probably all questioned the value of a relationship.
Some of us have reached the point where the return on our invest-
ment in a relationship seems like it's the opposite of what we antic-
ipated and hoped for. In all honesty, the pain, hurt, broken dreams,
abuse, and even cruelty can weigh very heavily on our hearts.
But I have never been able to forget these challenging words by
C. S. Lewis:

> There is no safe investment. To love at all is to be vulnerable.
> Love anything, and your heart will certainly be wrung and
> possibly broken. If you want to make sure of keeping it intact,
> you must give your heart to no one, not even to an animal. Wrap
> it carefully round with hobbies and little luxuries; avoid all
> entanglements; lock it up safe in the casket or coffin of your self-
> ishness. But in that casket—safe, dark, motionless, airless—it

will change. It will not be broken; it will become unbreakable, impenetrable, irredeemable.

What a poignant picture of love! If we lock our hearts away, they don't bloom and flourish; they shrivel up and become cold. So let's "love one another" and let His light shine . . . and stay out of that casket!

> *"To be loved but not known is comforting but superficial. To be known and not loved is our greatest fear. But to be fully known and truly loved is, well, a lot like being loved by God. It is what we need more than anything. It liberates us from pretense, humbles us out of our self-righteousness, and fortifies us for any difficulty life can throw at us."*
> ~ TIM KELLER

BE FEARLESS: *that which has the potential for greatest joy also has the potential for greatest pain. Such is the power of relationships. We must choose wisely, but we should prioritize building and nurturing relationships.*

ARE YOU WEARY?

*"Cast your burden on the Lord, and he will sustain you;
he will never permit the righteous to be moved."*
~ PSALM 55:22 (ESV)

Daily Meditation: Psalm 136, Psalm 62

On many restless nights, the word "tired" just isn't intense enough to adequately describe how we feel. That's why we have so many other creative words to express how tired we really are: drained, exhausted, done, empty, dead, fatigued, and the like. But here is some good news about God . . . our heavenly Father is not going to increase our burden when we come to Him. What's more, His "burden is light" (Matthew 11:30).

He cares about your big things and your little things. He cares about every single part of your life. As we approach our God, whether in prayer, in praise, or even in silence, the beautiful thing is that His door stands wide open, ready to welcome us in. We can come to Him with all of our fears, trials, and burdens. No penance needed. No gifts required. In fact, He wants you to come with empty hands, and in exchange He declares, "I will give you rest." I'll take that! While we rest, God restores, replenishes, and refocuses our hearts and minds. He doesn't rest! He never grows weary. We do, but He doesn't! Isn't that a comforting thought?

> *"There is hope for the helpless*
> *Rest for the weary*
> *Love for the broken heart*
> *There is grace and forgiveness*
> *Mercy and healing*
> *He'll meet you wherever you are*
> *Cry out to Jesus."*
> ~ THIRD DAY, "CRY OUT TO JESUS"

BE FEARLESS: *today you can rest in the knowledge that God is guiding you and waiting for you to lay your burdens down at His feet. Don't stress! God's got this. Rest in Him. He will help carry your burdens, freeing your mind to sleep peacefully at night! You need your rest, and God desires to give you holy, deep rest if you will only allow Him to help you.*

"BEING STILL" IS ACTUALLY POSSIBLE

"Be still and know that I am God."
—Psalm 46:10 (NIV)

Daily Meditation: Psalm 46, Exodus 14:14

Stillness. It's a difficult state to achieve in our everyday lives. Most mornings we as women feel overwhelmed with life and the responsibilities it holds, and yet this act of being still is of great value to us in our pursuit of physical, mental, relational, and spiritual health.

The first part of Psalm 37:7 says, "Be still before the Lord and wait patiently for him." We know what stillness is, but most of us aren't sure if we can actually experience it in our lives. How is it possible for us to be still when we have to balance all the responsibilities and pressures of family needs, work obligations, ministry commitments, and investments in friendships, not to mention that exhaustive everyday to-do list? I'm anxious just thinking about it all! In a world where it seems like no one else is stopping or being still, why, and especially how, can we expect to?

Let me encourage you to take the first step in your attempt at stillness by meditating on these truths:

He is God . . . and He is here for me.
He is God . . . and He is in control.
He is God . . . and He sees me and loves me.
He is God . . . and I don't have to be.

When I know and truly believe that *He* is God—and I am not—my perspective changes. The anxiety lessens. The fears recede. The darkness begins to break. And all of these changes then usher in a sense of calm, an ability to be still.

There's no denying that stillness is a challenge for all of us. But God knows it's possible, and He has given us the truth we need to cling to in order to experience it.

"In the silence of the heart God speaks.
~ MOTHER TERESA

BE FEARLESS: *Jesus exemplifies what it means to be still before God. He is never anxious, hurried, or too busy. Today, try to spend time being still before God. I believe that in this stillness we can really begin to "know" just how mighty our heavenly Father really is . . . and when we truly comprehend just how capable, strong, caring, and amazing He is, our lives change for the better!*

CRAZY LOVE

"And to know this love that surpasses knowledge—
that you may be filled to the measure of all the fullness of God."
~ EPHESIANS 3:19 (NIV)

Daily Meditation: Ephesians 3, Romans 8:37–39

One of the most enjoyable revelations I had recently was the realization of just how crazy God's love for me is. That's right: He loves us with a crazy love beyond our wildest dreams! (You may need to read that a second time!)

Here is what I mean, penned so well by author Gerald Bridges.

Any time that we are tempted to doubt God's love for us, we should go back to the Cross. We should reason somewhat in this fashion: If God loved me enough to give His Son to die for me when I was His enemy, surely He loves me enough to care for me now that I am His child. Having loved me to the ultimate extent at the Cross, He cannot possibly fail to love me in my times of adversity.

What will we be like when we are full of God's love? Is being full of God's love even possible? His "love that surpasses knowledge" is beyond comprehension. And I absolutely love it because that means he loves us when we are lost, confused, angry, and hurting. He loves us when we are depressed and discouraged. He loves us when we are joyful and content. He loves us in every circumstance, regardless of whether we feel lovable or not! God is love, and his extreme acts of love toward us should forever remove any doubts about His love for us!

> *"No matter what storm you face, you need*
> *to know that God loves you.*
> *He has not abandoned you."*
> ~ FRANKLIN GRAHAM

BE FEARLESS: *go ahead, let your mind take a pause. Sit on Father God's lap for just a second and tell Him thanks for loving you so much. We don't fully understand why He loves us so much, so well, and so completely, but right here and now we can cement in our hearts fact that His love for us is permanent … and amazing!*

SOMETHING SPECIAL

*"For you created my inmost being; you knit
me together in my mother's womb."*
—PSALM 139:13 (NIV)

Daily Meditation: Psalm 91:14, Jeremiah 1:5

My grandmother Helen used to knit blankets, Christmas ornaments, afghans, and kitchen towels. I have a special shelf in my closet with all those hand-knitted treasures she gave me over the years. They mean so much to me because they represent her tireless work. Her nimble fingers knit together the yarn into beautiful patterns. Knitting is an amazing skill that can transform an ordinary skein of yarn into an intricately designed pattern in a warm blanket. That is why it has always meant so much to me to know that God has "knit me together in my mother's womb." I am no accident; I am intricately designed. And so are you!

In addition, I know that whatever God knits together is His divine work. Each of us is not only a work of art, we are also specially designed. What's more, He has unique plans for each and every one of us. Everything God has created has a purpose, and that includes you and me. You have value—incredible value—in the eyes of our

Creator. Why? Simply because He created you! You are His beloved daughter. He took great joy in shaping you in your mother's womb, knowing exactly who He was designing you to be. You are a one-of-a-kind, limited-edition design, created for a unique purpose by your loving heavenly Father!

> *"We have only to be yielded, that is, willing,*
> *surrendered, and He will do the rest.*
> *He will make us according to the pattern for*
> *which, in His love, He designed us."*
> ~ PETER MARSHALL

BE FEARLESS: *the world wants to drag us down and make us feel weak, worthless, and of little or no value ... but those feelings aren't true! Remind yourself often of what really is true, and rest in this one fact: you are something special.*

NEVER ALONE

"Never will I leave you; never will I forsake you."
~ HEBREWS 13:5B (NIV)

Daily Meditation: Hebrews 13, 1 Samuel 12:22

It's funny how in a room full of people we can still feel alone. Maybe you've felt alone in the school cafeteria, on the school bus, in a classroom, at a dance hall, with a sports team, or at a mall. Even in a place where there are people everywhere, in the midst of all the laughter and chatter we can sometimes feel more alone and isolated then when we are by ourselves. We've all had our moments of feeling alone even when we are surrounded by other people, but with God you are never alone. Not ever! You always have an audience of one! Listen to Him speak to your heart right now. He declares that:

- He will *never* leave you.
- He will *never* forsake you.

When I'm deep in worry, these two "nevers" move me toward peace and joy and help me sleep at night. Yes, we need friends, but even friends cannot fully remove our feelings of being alone. Only our Father in heaven can do that. He is with us every moment of the day, walking beside us, holding our hands, giving us the strength to carry on. Friends are wonderful, but there are times when they leave you. Friends can forsake you. People you rely on may hurt you deeply. But God will never abandon you. Even when you can't feel Him, He is still there! He longs to take you in his arms and comfort you. You are His daughter, His precious child! He will always be there for you when you need Him.

> *"Snuggle in God's arms. When you are*
> *hurting, when you feel lonely, left out.*
> *Let Him cradle you, comfort you, reassure you*
> *of His all-sufficient power and love."*
> ~ KAY ARTHUR

BE FEARLESS: *peace, not to mention boldness, comes when I realize that His hand is always in mine. We are not—and never can be—alone. His words are true. You are safe. Go ahead, cling to His hand!*

YOU BE YOU

"But thanks be to God, who always leads us as captives in Christ's triumphal procession and uses us to spread the aroma of the knowledge of him everywhere."
~ 2 CORINTHIANS 2:14 (NIV)

Daily Meditation: Psalm 27, 2 Corinthians 2

Do you ever feel like you're nothing special? Do you wonder why, out of all the people in the world, God would ever want to use you in His plan? You may feel like you're not important, but God has a plan for your life, and He loves to use people like you and me! He channels His love and grace through us to those around us. You may not realize it, but you're a witness for God in every moment of your life. What have others seen in you today?

You are a messenger to those around you: your kids, your husband, your coworkers, your friends, and more. Paul writes that we should be "the aroma of the knowledge of him."

Simply letting Christ be at work in you is more than enough. You don't have to be famous, and you don't have to be "the best." All you need is to be you, wholly surrendered to God and letting His aroma flow through you. Sweet scents permeate every nook and cranny, and your life can be a fragrant perfume that permeates the lives of those around you. The Holy Spirit flows through you as you relax and live life as His daughter.

Just be you. You may not have all the answers. You may not even know the right questions, but you being you is all you need to be. I've seen it time and time again: when women, already surrendered to God, simply go about living life, it's like a magnet! The hungry, the hurting, and the lost are drawn to their light. Like perfume, the aroma of Him surrounds you.

> *"The perfection of Christian character*
> *depends wholly upon the grace and strength found alone in God."*
> ~ ELLEN G. WHITE

———————

BE FEARLESS: *the battle to be ourselves, free in Christ, has already been fought and won at the cross. Jesus paid the price and broke open the prison doors, so now we can walk in freedom as we let His perfume spread throughout the world. You are free. There are no chains. You be you!*

REPEAT THE GOOD

"I will never forget your precepts, for by
them you have preserved my life."
~ PSALM 119:93 (NIV)

Daily Meditation: Psalm 119:9−16, 2 Corinthians 3

Do you ever have trouble remembering things? I know I do, and it drives me nuts!
But I've found that the best way to ensure that I remember something is to repeat it in my mind, write it down, or tell it to someone else and ask them to remind me about it.

I love the Psalms because they are constantly reminding me of God's goodness, truth, life, hope, and love. David repeats the truths of God's love over and over, cementing them in his mind and in mine. My hope is that "I will never forget your precepts" but that rather, through daily study I will remember everything I read from God's precious word!

So how can you always keep God's precepts in the forefront of your mind? By repeating them! Write them down. Journal about what you are learning. Discuss with a friend the scriptures you are reading. Engross yourself in the word of God to the point that you are living out the truths of scripture without even thinking about it! When we spend time around others, we start to emulate their characteristics, and the same thing happens when we spend time with God. Repeat the good. Live your life the way God tells you to! Think about his word; meditate on it and live out loud!

> *"Living is like tearing through a museum.*
> *Not until later do you really start*
> *absorbing what you saw, thinking about it,*
> *looking it up in a book, and remembering—*
> *because you can't take it in all at once."*
> ~ AUDREY HEPBURN

Let's do what it takes to not forget his precepts. Let's hide them in our hearts and live them out in our lives.

———————

BE FEARLESS: *it is sad to think how fast we forget the very words that bring us life. But now I believe you're motivated to remember and apply them! Let's focus today on hiding the words of scripture in our hearts. Let's make it our goal to absorb them and never let them go. The amazing thing about hiding His words in our lives is that it brings us life and freedom!*

DOING CRAZY THINGS

"Trust in the Lord with all your heart and
lean not on your own understanding;
in all your ways submit to him, and he
will make your paths straight."
~ Proverbs 3:5–6 (NIV)

Daily Meditation: Genesis 7, John 2:1–12

As the missionary stepped off the bus in Bangladesh, she was immediately accosted by two people begging for money. Their sad tale was that they needed money (about $30) from her so they could return home. The missionary only had about $35 cash on her. "What do I do, God?" she quickly prayed. Oddly enough, she felt she should give them what they asked. Handing over most of her money certainly qualified as a crazy thing to do but she did it anyway, trusting God. The appreciative couple disappeared to buy bus tickets.

As she turned and walked around the back of bus, a man stepped out with a knife and demanded, "Give me all your money!" She smiled and joyfully gave him all she had … a mere $5.

We do not always see the logic behind the seemingly crazy things we feel challenged to do. Sometimes the choice to "lean not on your own understanding" is not an easy one to make, but why shouldn't we? We trust Him with our futures; we can certainly trust Him with our daily lives! In fact, I find that it makes things easier. I don't know everything, and that's okay, because God does.

Think about it. Many of the stories we love to tell from the Bible are, for lack of a better term, totally crazy! Put hundreds of wild animals in an enclosed space and prepare for a massive flood— when such a thing has never happened before? Crazy! But Noah did it anyway. Pour water into jars to serve at a wedding when the guests ask for wine? Crazy! But when the servants did what Jesus told them to, they got to witness Jesus's first earthly miracle. God loves working through things that we think are crazy, so go ahead. If you feel God's call on your life to go and do something that seems strange, listen to the promptings of the Holy Spirit. You never know when God will use something crazy to turn your life upside down in an amazing way!

"Never be afraid to trust an unknown future to a known God."
~ CORRIE TEN BOOM

BE FEARLESS: *God often starts with "slightly crazy," moves on to "crazy," and follows that with "really crazy," so be patient with yourself as you walk into deeper waters. The end result with God is always crazy good!*

JUST ACCEPT IT

"May our Lord Jesus Christ himself and God our Father,
who loved us and by his grace gave us eternal
encouragement and good hope,
encourage your hearts and strengthen you
in every good deed and word."
~ 2 THESSALONIANS 2:16 (NIV)

Daily Meditation: Psalm 86, John 3:1–21

God loves you . . . a lot! It's time to accept the fact that we are utterly, completely, and permanently loved by God. That is the foundation of all love, including love of self, love of others, and love of God. Now if that isn't "eternal encouragement and good hope," I don't know what is! There is nothing we need to do and nothing we need to say in order to gain God's love and acceptance. We just need to embrace his mercy and revel in the love He showers upon us.

Sadly, that isn't so easy. Incredibly few believers live each day as if the God of the universe has great affection for them. Why? Because 2,000 years of religious tradition have drilled into us the mistaken notion that God's love is something we earn; that if we do what pleases him, he loves us, and if we don't, he doesn't. Giving up that belief isn't easy. Moving from a performance-based religious ethic toward a relationship deeply rooted in the Father's affection is no small transition.

How do we start recognizing and believing that this love of God is within our grasp? The process begins by simply accepting His love. We don't have to do anything—we can't do anything—to make Him love us. Love is not earned; it is given. And God gives it freely, without any cost. What an amazing truth! How different would your life look if you lived every day as though you truly believed that you were loved unconditionally by the all-powerful God of the universe?

> *"God loves each of us as if there were only one of us."*
> ~ SAINT AUGUSTINE

BE FEARLESS: *that you are fully loved and wanted by your heavenly Father is a fact. Embrace it. Embrace him. Accept His love! Breathe in His affection. Make this your new reality! Thankfully, this new life never fades, and it can't be returned. It's yours now, forever!*

THE HABIT OF LISTENING

"For the word of God is alive and active.
Sharper than any double-edged sword,
it penetrates even to dividing soul and spirit, joints and marrow;
it judges the thoughts and attitudes of the heart."
~ HEBREWS 4:12 (NIV)

Daily Meditation: I Samuel 3, I Kings 19:11–13

Have you ever found yourself in a conversation that feels more like a monologue? It can be frustrating to try to have a "conversation" when the other person won't let you get a word in edgewise! Or perhaps you are the one doing all the talking while the other person is just nodding along. Too often, our conversations with God fall into this latter category. It is wonderful to talk to God, but I have found something even better than talking *to* God. It is hearing Him speak to me! We miss so much when we talk with God, because we are the ones doing all the talking without truly taking time to listen to what God wants to say to *us*.

Why is it so important to listen to God? Because "the word of God is alive and active." It is sharp, it cuts through every issue, and it brings us incredible clarity and life. It is unstoppable! We pray for answers, but often we don't stop to truly listen for God to speak into our lives.

Quite frankly, I want the power of God's word working in my life. We all do, which means we need to make it a daily habit to listen. By His Spirit, God speaks through scriptures, thoughts, words, friends, and neighbors. We can certainly talk to God, too, but let's make it more of a dialogue than a monologue. Let Him speak to you through His word, through other people, through promptings of the Spirit. He wants to speak to us, but we must be listening.

Speak, Lord, your servant hears—but the question is . . . are we listening?

> *"Our failure to hear His voice when we want*
> *to is due to the fact that we do not in general*
> *want to hear it, that we want it only*
> *when we think we need it."*
> ~ DALLAS WILLARD

BE FEARLESS: *I love that God is not silent. He speaks, and every word brings me life. I want to turn my ear to hear even more! Let's focus today on truly listening. Speak, Lord! Your servant listens.*

GO AHEAD, FORGIVE YOURSELF

"And forgive us our debts, as we also have forgiven our debtors."
~ MATTHEW 6:12 (NIV)

Daily Meditation: Psalm 32, Colossians 1

"I forgive you" may be one of the most challenging English sentences to say—or to come to terms with if an apology never comes. It can be very difficult to forgive others when they have wronged us, and sometimes the hardest person for us to forgive is actually...ourselves. Instead of truly letting go, we replay things over and over in our minds, especially when it comes to self-forgiveness. As strange as it seems, it is often easier to forgive other people than to forgive ourselves.

But God doesn't want to us to live in self-loathing and unforgiveness. If the God of the entire universe has forgiven us, why should we hold on to our debts and refuse to forgive? When Jesus taught us how to pray, saying "forgive us our debts, as we also have forgiven our debtors," He was, among other things, making it plain that we need to forgive ourselves as well as others. The sad thing is that we usually don't do it! We have in our hands the power to forgive ourselves, but often we simply refuse to accept that we can be forgiven.

Granting forgiveness allows room for growth, freedom, and mercy. You have that power, so use it wisely and forgive yourself. Forgiveness breaks the chains that bind you to a difficult person or painful situation. Set yourself free through forgiveness!

Interestingly, the most loving, genuine, strong, and caring people I know are also the ones who know how to forgive themselves. I want that. Don't you?

> *"There is no lasting joy in forgiveness if it*
> *doesn't include forgiving yourself."*
> ~ R. T. KENDALL

BE FEARLESS: *all forgiveness comes with a price tag of grace and mercy. Give yourself the same forgiveness that you give others. There is grace and mercy for you as well. We can forgive ourselves because he forgave us. Go on, forgive yourself. If God forgave you, you can too!*

NOT-SO-HIDDEN BLESSINGS

"Every good and perfect gift is from above, coming down from the
Father of the heavenly lights,
who does not change like shifting shadows."
~ JAMES 1:17 (NIV)

Daily Meditation: Jeremiah 17:7–8, Psalm 34

Have you seen God today? Maybe you think you haven't, but look around you.
James writes that "every good and perfect gift" comes from the
Father! What has blessed you today? Was it a hug, a random phone
call from a friend, a text, or the song you really needed to hear on
the radio? Have you thought about what God drops on us every day?

God loves to bless you in little ways throughout the day. We may
not even realize it because we're not looking, but when we truly
look around us and pay attention to all the little blessings we experience in life, we can start to clearly see God's hand at work in our
everyday lives. There is an old hymn that proclaims "Count your
blessings, name them one by one. Count your blessings, see what
God has done! Count your blessings, name them one by one, and it
will surprise you what the Lord has done!"

As I look around me, His gifts are evident! They all feel like our Father smiling down. Even that free cup of weak coffee, that handwritten note from a child, or that burly guy on the plane who helps jam your bag in the overhead compartment, these little blessings can turn your day from dull and depressing to full of joy!

The good news is that God "does not change," so keep your eyes wide open to see His not-so-hidden blessings.

"There are two ways to live: you can live as if nothing is a miracle; you can live as if everything is a miracle."
~ ALBERT EINSTEIN

BE FEARLESS: *I don't think we're even aware of how many good and perfect gifts God sends our way. I wish we could see them clearly, for then we would marvel. The more you see, the more you will know. Let's count our blessings today!*

YOU CAN TRUST HIM

"He is the Rock, his works are perfect, and all his ways are just.
A faithful God who does no wrong, upright and just is he."
~ DEUTERONOMY 32:4 (NIV)

Daily Meditation: Isaiah 26:1–19, Psalm 20

Trust is not something that comes easily to most of us, especially when we have been hurt. Maybe it is the result of what we have learned or unlearned, but full-on trust is hard to give. We want to feel safe, and we believe that if we don't trust we won't get hurt, but if we refuse to trust, we run the risk of getting hurt in a different way. How can we learn to build trust? We can start by placing our trust in the One who will never let us down.

God is worthy of our trust. After all, He is "faithful" and He "does no wrong, upright and just is he." There is no one safer in whom to place our trust. Why is it then that we struggle so much with turning our lives over to Him? We have ample evidence of God's trustworthiness, and yet trusting Him is admittedly one of—if not the most—challenging things we will ever face in life. Why? Because we want to be in control and placing our trust in someone else means relinquishing at least some measure of control.

The more closely I looked, the more I noticed God's many obvious acts of love for me. They were everywhere, and yet it still seemed hard to trust … but then it clicked! I trust God to the extent that my heart knows He loves me! The more I revel in His love for me, the more I realize how much I trust Him. It isn't even something I try to do; I can't help it! God is love. It's no coincidence that everything comes back to that.

> "We must cease striving and trust God to provide
> what He thinks is best and in whatever time
> He chooses to make it available. But this kind
> of trusting doesn't come naturally.
> It's a spiritual crisis of the will in which
> we must choose to exercise faith."
> ~ CHARLES R. SWINDOLL

———————

BE FEARLESS: *we feel bad when we don't trust God as we know we should, but trust isn't something we can buy, much less self-generate. It is a byproduct of knowing how much we are loved. And His love is limitless, so let yourself trust again by placing your faith in Him.*

COPYCAT

"Be imitators of me, as I am of Christ."
~ 1 CORINTHIANS 11:1 (ESV)

Daily Meditation: Philippians 4:8–9, Mark 8:34–38

Whose life do you want to copy? In the age of social media where people flaunt, brag, and strut their stuff, all in an effort to boost their ratings, likes, and subscribers, sometimes it feels like everyone out there has a better life than I do! I start to think, *Oh, if only my life were like hers. It looks like she has it all together. Look at those amazing pictures she's posting!* And as I wish for the life someone else has, I can grow discontented with my own life and start trying to imitate the lives I see other people living online.

But those online lives show only people's highlights. No one posts pictures of their kids throwing tantrums, their bad hair days, their house in a state of chaos. We need to take a step back and remember that God made us—flaws and all!—just the way we are. And stepping back reminds me that the people I most want to be like, the people I truly want to copy, are not the popular people who live in a bubble of temporary fame. On the contrary, I want to copy people who are loving, kind, gentle, and humble; the people who have poured into my life and shown me God's love. They are so full of God's life that it bubbles out of their lives and right into mine! That is a legacy worthy copying.

After all, it is God's kindness that leads us to repentance. He could easily have demanded our repentance, but God doesn't force His children. He lets us choose to change, and we do so because we want to as a response to His kindness. A legacy worth leaving is one worth copying, so go ahead lift your head high. Boldly be yourself! And lead by example. It's okay to have flaws; everyone does. But what makes a life worth copying is the beauty that shines from within—the beauty that comes from a godly, holy life. That's what we really want to be: lives that reflect Jesus. After all, it's Jesus's life that we ultimately want to copy.

> *"You're born an original; don't die a copy."*
> ~ JOHN MASON

BE FEARLESS: *you are free to be you, to be whole, to be humble, and to love people. That's how people want to be, and it's what they want to copy. Live a life worthy of copying, and be a testament to all.*

HAPPY, HOLY, OR BOTH?

"And by that will, we have been made holy through the sacrifice
of the body of Jesus Christ once for all."
~ HEBREWS 10:10 (NIV)

Daily Meditation: Psalm 65, 1 Peter 1

What do you enjoy doing? What makes you happy? Is it something that is lasting and memorable, or is it a temporary "happiness fix"? We all like to be happy. We want to be happy. We enjoy being happy. Happiness is fun! Nobody would argue with that. But when it comes to being happy or being holy, which do you choose? Can you be happy *and* holy?

The real problem comes when the things we believe make us happy are, as much as we don't want to admit it, sinful. Maybe it's that TV show you're hooked on that glorifies things contrary to God's word. Maybe it's that "guilty pleasure" that you like to sweep under the rug. Maybe it's a relationship you know is unhealthy. "But it makes me happy!" we cry. Happy for a time? Perhaps. But is it a lasting happiness? If we're honest with ourselves, the answer is no.

When does "harmless" become "harmful"? When does happiness become an idol that we pursue at the expense of holiness? We must be careful not to let what we think will make us happy get in the way of what God dictates we must do to be holy. Ultimately, true happiness comes not from the worldly things that we think will make us happy, but from God's gifts in our lives. Living a life fully devoted to God and following His commands leads to a life that is richer, fuller, and happier than anything we can imagine! Psalm 37:4 (NKJV) says to "delight yourself also in the Lord and he shall give you the desires of your heart." God wants us to be happy, and when we delight ourselves in Him, He gives us the best gift of all—Himself.

So yes, we *can* be happy and holy. We just have to find our happiness in the right place: in God!

> *"Happiness comes from holiness. You can't truly be*
> *happy unless you're hungry for Jesus Christ."*
> ~ DAVID JEREMIAH

BE FEARLESS: *most people don't get the whole holiness thing, but God does, and that is all that matters. It is part of His plan for us. Holiness brings life, peace, and true happiness. When you choose holiness, you get happiness as a result. With God, you can have both!*

RENEWAL IS COMING

*"In her deep anguish Hannah prayed to
the Lord, weeping bitterly."*
~ 1 SAMUEL 1:10 (NIV)

Daily Meditation: 1 Samuel 1, 1 Samuel 2:1–21

Have you ever longed for something so deeply that you felt it in your very soul?
Have you ever experienced pain pouring out of you in anguish over
a desperate desire of your heart? In 1 Samuel 1, the Bible tells us
of one woman who felt that kind of deep, searing pain. Hannah
desperately wanted a baby, but she couldn't get pregnant. Year after
year she prayed, but she did not conceive. For a time her prayers
went unanswered.

In the depths of her despair she "prayed to the Lord, weeping
bitterly." At her wit's end, she vowed to dedicate the child to God
if only she could have a baby. The intensity of her grief and the
fervency of her silent prayers were so great that the priest thought
she was drunk! But her story does not end in sorrow. The priest
told Hannah that God would grant her request, and He did.

It is hard to imagine all the stress and pent-up emotions Hannah
endured, but God took care of her. She did become pregnant and

went on to dedicate her son Samuel to the Lord as she had vowed. And Samuel went on to make history, doing great works for God.

There is one amazing detail about this story that I absolutely love: Hannah went on to bear three more sons and two daughters! Her prayers were not answered immediately, but God honored her faithfulness and showered her with blessings beyond her requests. His plans for her were greater than her own—and the same is true for us.

Your Father knows your needs. Renewal is coming!

"Revival is not just an emotional touch; it's a complete takeover!"
~ NANCY DEMOSS WOLGEMUTH

BE FEARLESS: *when we have a desperate desire, we want it fulfilled right away. We want our prayers answered immediately, but sometimes waiting is required. Hannah prayed year after year before finally experiencing the answer to her prayers. Waiting can be difficult and living with unanswered prayers is stressful . . . unless we make the choice to surrender and fully trust God to satisfy our longings in His time!*

OUR SOURCE OF STRENGTH

*"David was greatly distressed because the
men were talking of stoning him;
each one was bitter in spirit because of his sons and daughters.
But David found strength in the Lord his God."*
~ 1 SAMUEL 30:6 (NIV)

Daily Meditation: 1 Samuel 30, Exodus 15:2

To say that David "was greatly distressed" would be putting it mildly. These men, his friends and fellow soldiers, had lost everything: their wives, their children, and their homes. Now they wanted someone to blame. I don't know about you, but I have never met anyone who can personally relate to the threat of being stoned. But you may have had friends turn on you. You may have been blamed for tragedies that occurred because you weren't there to stop them. You may have felt guilt, sorrow, or pain when surrounded by people you care about who are bitter and angry.

Yet in the midst of all his darkness and grief, notice what David did. He "found strength in the Lord his God," which, based on what we know about David, most likely meant that he was on his knees crying out to God. When everyone turned against him, he turned to the One who would never leave him nor forsake him. And in those moments, God gave him the answer he needed.

When you feel helpless and friendless, turn your face toward God! Pray without ceasing. Devote yourself to praising God even in the midst of hardship. Lock yourself in your room, car, or closet so you can turn your whole heart to God. Get lost in Him and strengthen yourself in the Lord. That's when His strength will become yours.

> *"Stress makes you believe that everything has to happen right now.*
> *Faith reassures you that everything will happen in God's timing."*
> ~ AUTHOR UNKNOWN

BE FEARLESS: *stepping back and taking time away from a difficult situation is not a sign of weakness; it is a sign of strength. God's power is at work in us even when everyone turns against us. We tap into His strength when we stop to praise Him. Strengthen yourself in the Lord today and every day.*

CHOOSE TO BELIEVE

"...so that at the name of Jesus every knee will bow—
of those who are in heaven and on earth and under the earth—"
~ Philippians 2:10 (HCSB)

Daily Meditation: Philippians 2, 1 Timothy 4:10

Belief is a choice. When our circumstances curl back like a 60-foot wave, about to wash over and destroy us, we must make the choice to believe that, despite the chaos around us, God is still in control. When life is falling apart and problems and challenges threaten to consume us, even if we need to close our eyes and hold our breath, we must declare the truth that:

- God is way more powerful than my problem.
- God is omnipotent; my challenges are not.
- God is bigger than my situation.
- God is higher than my wall.
- Good will come from this yet.

The Bible tells us that one day, "every knee will bow" at the name of Jesus. He is victorious over all; there are no circumstances in life that are too hard for Him, no obstacles that He cannot surmount. He is the one who is in control because He is the one true God. There is no other. Let Him have the authority to reign in your life. Stand strong in Him, your King of kings and your Lord of lords!

> *"There are three stages in the work of*
> *God: impossible, difficult, done."*
> ~ JAMES HUDSON TAYLOR

BE FEARLESS: *God has a miraculous way of bringing good out of terrible circumstances. No matter what you may be facing, you can choose to put your faith and trust in Him. He is always with you—every step of the way!*

HE HOLDS MY HEART

"Weeping may stay for the night, but
rejoicing comes in the morning."
~ PSALM 30:5B (NIV)

Daily Meditation: Psalm 73:21–28, Ecclesiastes 1:3–11

"God needed another angel."
"They are better off now."

I really struggle with these kinds of glib answers to some of the incredibly painful situations we experience in life. People may mean well, but sometimes the condolences they offer us can feel shallow, superficial, and fake. Their words are meant to comfort, but they often leave us more grieved, sad, empty, or angry.

In some ways, it hurts all the more because they insinuate that God took away our loved one because He *needed* something. These trite statements can make us cry out even more, "Why, God?"

Yes, there is pain and loss in life, and there will be times of grief. It is not wrong to grieve, for grieving is a statement that you have loved deeply. But in the midst of our pain and suffering, we can still find hope and comfort in God's word. The sorrow will not last forever, for "rejoicing comes in the morning." God will one day turn our mourning into dancing. We can be confident of that. Even when our pain is overwhelming, God is still present in the midst of it all. Feel His embrace and ask Him to hold your heart. You will get through this.

> *"Our vision is so limited we can hardly imagine a love that does not show itself in protection from suffering.... The love of God did not protect His own Son.... He will not necessarily protect us—not from anything it takes to make us like His Son. A lot of hammering and chiseling and purifying by fire will have to go into the process."*
> ~ ELISABETH ELLIOT

BE FEARLESS: *the pain may feel like it will last forever, but in time it will get better. The morning always comes. God's divine comfort can ease even the most painful losses. He knows our grief and will mourn alongside us. When your sorrow seems overwhelming and you don't know how you are going to face another day, cling to Jesus as your source of strength and hope. He knows your pain and will walk with you all the way through it.*

PURPOSELY UNBALANCED

"Come to me, all you who are weary and
burdened, and I will give you rest."
~ MATTHEW 11:28 (NIV)

Daily Meditation: 1 Corinthians 10:13, Psalm 7

What do you turn to when you are overwhelmed, tired, frustrated, hurt, or
exhausted? Jesus is calling. You may be too busy to hear Him, but
He is simply saying, "Come to me." So run to Him! Don't try to
fight through the stress and chaos on your own. Let Him hold you
and remind you that He is with you. He declares, "I will give you
rest." When we are overwhelmed and overworked and life feels
continually off balance, He will give us the gift we so desperately
need—rest!

When I came to the realization that my Father is always giving
me far more than I give to Him, another revelation occurred in
my heart … God does this on purpose! God gives us more than we
can handle in our *own* strength, but never more than we can handle
in *His* strength. When we are knocked off balance we are forced
to turn back to Him, and it is God who steadies us. It is God who
gives us rest.

"God wants us to know Him deeply because He
knows what knowing Him will do for us."
~ PETER V. DEISON

———————————

BE FEARLESS: *I am so thankful that I can run to God in times of need. He
welcomes me, and He welcomes you too! In the tough times, He is there—with you,
for you, and ready to abundantly give you the rest you need.*

MIND GAMES

"Sow for yourselves righteousness; reap steadfast love;
break up your fallow ground,
for it is the time to seek the Lord, that he may
come and rain righteousness upon you."

~ HOSEA 10:12 (ESV)

Daily Meditation: Joshua 6, Psalm 26:2

Sow a thought, reap an action. Sow an action, reap a habit. Sow a habit, reap char-
acter. Sow character, reap a destiny.

Our thoughts influence us at the deepest level. Paul was aware
of this when he wrote, "Finally, brothers and sisters, whatever is
true, whatever is noble, whatever is right, whatever is pure, whatever is lovely, whatever is admirable—if anything is excellent or
praiseworthy—think about such things" (Philippians 4:8, NIV).

It is easy for us to lose track of our thought life and develop
angry or hateful thoughts. But allowing ourselves to slip into the
habit of letting our thoughts run wild can take a serious toll on
our lives. Even though thoughts cannot be seen, they can have defi-
nite consequences if we let them influence our actions. How do we
break such negative cycles? By setting our "minds on things above,
not on earthly things" (Colossians 3:2, NIV).

That may be hard to do, but little by little, one small thought at a time, we can learn to discipline our minds and control our thoughts. How? By walking with God and sowing the right seeds—the right thoughts—which will inevitably bring the right harvest. No more mind games. Let's fix our gaze on Him.

> *"Your mind will quit a thousand times before your*
> *body will. Feel the fear and do it anyway!"*
> ~ AUTHOR UNKNOWN

BE FEARLESS: *thoughts are so small, yet they direct our lives in major ways. No one else on the planet has the power to control your thoughts. They are your own, for better or for worse. So decide today to set your mind on the things of heaven, not the things of earth. Heavenly thinking will change your life!*

THROUGH GOD'S EYES

"For the entire law is fulfilled in keeping this one
command: 'Love your neighbor as yourself.'"
~ GALATIANS 5:14 (NIV)

Daily Meditation: Galatians 5, Matthew 5:43–48

God tells us to "love your neighbor as yourself," but what if we don't even like ourselves? Maybe that's because of some annoying physical characteristic; a challenging relational situation at work, in our family, or with a friend; regret over a past mistake; or sadness about the gap between where we are and where we thought we'd be at this point in life. Maybe we just don't feel as though we're worth anything. Maybe we play the comparison game, looking at other people and envying their "perfect" lives. But what if you saw yourself the way God sees you? When He looks at you He sees His beautiful daughter, someone worth dying for!

That's right. Stop being so hard on yourself! Stop being so critical of God's creation! Remember who you are because of whose you are. Take time to accept God's love and affection for you. Forgive yourself if you need to but focus on receiving the limitless love He has for you. Recognize your value in the eyes of

God. Let yourself be loved. God loved you so much He went to Calvary for *you*.

His love for us is beyond anything we can fathom and because of that, we can start learning to love ourselves; not pridefully but in humility, recognizing and internalizing the incredible love we've been given. We must accept His love for us and let that love seep into every nook and cranny of our lives. Then it will inevitably and unashamedly overflow into the lives of those around us.

> *"Look for yourself and you will find loneliness and despair.*
> *But look for Christ and you will find Him and everything else"*
> ~ C. S. LEWIS

BE FEARLESS: *the truth is we can only love to the degree that we know we are loved. Loving others will flow out as a result. We cannot pour from an empty cup. However, when we allow our cup to keep being filled by God's unlimited love and strength, we are able to pour into others without running empty ourselves. So go ahead, fill 'er up!*

JUST WALK AWAY

Therefore, since we are surrounded by
such a great cloud of witnesses,
let us throw off everything that hinders
and the sin that so easily entangles.
And let us run with perseverance the race marked out for us,"
~ HEBREWS 12:1 (NIV)

Daily Meditation: Matthew 4:1–17, Galatians 6:1–10

"But no one's watching. No one would know. It isn't that big of a deal. "

We tell ourselves so many lies to justify succumbing to temptation. Walking away from a temptation (especially when nobody is watching) can really be hard! What's interesting is that we usually know what is right. Often we even *want* to do what is right, so what's our problem? Scripture makes it plain when it says, "Throw off everything that hinders and the sin that so easily entangles." Sadly, the "so easily" part is very true. It's almost always easier to get ourselves into trouble than out of it!

Be bold. Let your courage rise up within you. Be mighty! Choose to be the real you . . . and walk away from temptation's snare! And as you are walking away, you will be filled with power from on high.

God will meet you, empower you, and help you stand firm against temptation!

> *"There is no easy walk to freedom anywhere,*
> *and many of us will have to pass*
> *through the valley of the shadow of death again and again*
> *before we reach the mountaintop of our desires."*
> ~ NELSON MANDELA

———————————

BE FEARLESS: *sometimes just walking away isn't enough; you may have to run! Don't stop to think about it, don't stop to look at it, don't stop to weigh the pros and cons of giving in to a temptation—flee from temptation and run to God! He is with you through the fiercest of trials and temptations. With His strength, you can walk away. You are a winner. Keep on walking!*

THROW OFF THE CHAINS

*"It is for freedom that Christ has set us free. Stand firm, then,
and do not let yourselves be burdened again by a yoke of slavery."*
~ GALATIANS 5:1 (NIV)

Daily Meditation: Romans 6:18, Acts 13:38–39

My dad loved the circus. Back in those days, elephants were often tied to a small stake in the center of the ring with only a rope to secure them to their post. Though the elephants obviously had the physical strength to rip themselves free and go rampaging down the street, flipping cars and squashing people, they never did. Ever wonder why? I did, and I learned that as babies, circus elephants were trained by being chained to a massive stake driven deep into the ground. After countless tries to pull free the young elephants gave up, and soon all it took to keep them in place was a simple rope and a wooden post. In their minds, they were as firmly restrained as if they'd been bound with a thick iron chain.

"It's impossible … it's impossible. I can't do it. I've tried a million times and it's no use. There is nothing I can do. I'm stuck. This is my lot in life."

Yet nothing could be further from the truth. The elephant could break free anytime, and so can you and I! We just have to decide to break free—free from the "slavery" of working hard to earn God's love; free from the burden of always trying to measure up; free from the feeling that we have to be perfect (or even "good enough"); free from the mental chains that drag us down. God knows the truth about us and our lives, and that is why He encourages us, "Do not let yourselves be burdened again by a yoke of slavery."

He knows you can break free from the chains because He has already made you strong enough to do it!

> *"Man is free at the moment he wishes to be."*
> ~ VOLTAIRE

BE FEARLESS: *God sees us not only for who we are, but for who we can become. He encourages us to fight for our freedom because we truly are free. He wants us to be free even more than we do. That is our God!*

GET IT, GIRL!

*"Then Jesus said to her, 'Woman, you have
great faith! Your request is granted.'
And her daughter was healed at that moment."*

~ MATTHEW 15:28 (NIV)

Daily Meditation: Matthew 15:21–28, Luke 11:5–13

Imagine being praised by Jesus for having great faith. Remember the story of the
woman who was begging Jesus for her daughter's healing? Jesus told
her, "You have great faith!" and he added, "Your request is granted."
Can you imagine that?

This woman was a fighter. She would not take no for an answer!
When she initially asked Jesus to heal her daughter He ignored her,
but instead of giving up she kept on asking. His disciples begged
Jesus to make her leave, and Jesus even told her bluntly that He
came only for the "lost sheep of Israel" (vs. 24). But she didn't leave.
She fell to her knees and begged again, and Jesus pushed back as
well, explaining that it was not right to "take the children's bread
and toss it to the dogs" (vs. 26).

What type of woman would stand up to Jesus, God's only Son
and savior of the world, and say to his face, "Yes, Lord, *but...?!?*" She

refused to be denied. She would not let go until He met her need, and He did!

> *Get it, girl! Keep the faith, and press in. He is there to meet you.*
> *"Faith is deliberate confidence in the character of God*
> *whose ways you may not understand at the time."*
> ~ OSWALD CHAMBERS

———————

BE FEARLESS: *hold on for what you believe, want, and need from Him. Like a pit bull, refuse to let go. Keep asking, keep seeking, keep knocking! That is faith! Get it, girl! Plant yourself at the feet of the One who is God, who is love, and who is your Father.*

PLANT ME DEEP

"That person is like a tree planted by streams of water,
which yields its fruit in season and whose leaf does
not wither—whatever they do prospers."
~ PSALM 1:3 (NIV)

Daily Meditation: Psalm 1, Jeremiah 17:5–8

I don't have a natural green thumb at all. And I've tried! What about you? Have you ever planted several tiny tomato plants together in one small pot, watered them well, taken care of them, and brooded over them, only to see them turn into midget plants that bear no tomatoes at all? But pop one of those tiny tomato plants out of that crowded pot and stick it in the ground with plenty of room to grow and boom! You'll soon be harvesting a lot of tomatoes!

Room to grow is a requirement for healthy living. When it comes to our walk with God, I believe we all desire to be a "tree planted by streams of water," because we know that means we'll have "fruit in season" and a leaf that "does not wither."

If God is going to plant me, then I say, "Plant me deep!" I don't want to disrupt the process or limit the outcome. Nobody has a green thumb like God's. He can bring dead plants to life. It may take time and it may take work, but I'll accept that. I want life and fruit. Plant me deep!

> *"So neither the one who plants nor the one who waters is anything,*
> *but only God, who makes things grow."*
> ~ I Corinthians 3:7 (NIV)

———————————

BE FEARLESS: *plants seldom grow fast, and trees certainly do not. Stay anchored and rooted in Christ. He is your stream of living water. And if it takes time, so be it. Let your Father lovingly set your roots deep in the ground. His touch will always bring life!*

CALL ME WHAT YOU WILL

"Because the Sovereign Lord helps me, I will not be disgraced.
Therefore have I set my face like flint, and
I know I will not be put to shame."
~ ISAIAH 50:7 (NIV)

Daily Meditation: Isaiah 50, Exodus 34:29–35

As daughters of God, shame has no place in our lives. He loves us deeply and unconditionally. And the more we understand His grace, the more bold and fearless our lives become. We can be confident in our identities as daughters of God.

Set your "face like flint," and do not worry about what anyone else dares to think, say, or do. Focus wholly on following God and doing the Father's will. Bask in His love. Your life will reflect a holy confidence! With God as your father, you can be:

- Bold
- Courageous
- Strong
- Powerful
- Beautiful
- Amazing

How? By simply being you. You reflect the characteristics of those you spend time with, so spend time with God. Then His love and confidence will burst out of you and overflow! I love the story about Moses speaking with God on Mount Sinai; when Moses came back down from the mountain his face shone, simply from being in the presence of God. Fix your gaze on God and, like Moses, you will shine! And when you have set your face like flint, don't look back.

> *"No one can make you feel inferior without your consent."*
> ~ ELEANOR ROOSEVELT

BE FEARLESS: *call it what you want, there is a time and a place to not back down. Spend time with the Father and you'll be able to walk in confidence and boldness, secure in the knowledge that you are God's precious daughter! Then the world had better watch out, because you—the daughter of the King—are coming through.*

DEFINE YOURSELF CORRECTLY

"Save me, for I am yours; I have sought out your precepts."
~ PSALM 119:94 (NIV)

Daily Meditation: Psalm 119:89−96, Ephesians 1:1−14

"Save me, God! Please, God, show up! Rescue me, us, our family."

How many times have you cried out to God in desperation? And have you ever wondered if He's even listening? We may doubt who we really are in Christ, and we may doubt that He hears us. But He does. He is always listening, and He wants us to come to Him.

"Who am I? What value do I have? Am I important to you, to me, to God, to others?"

Because I know that "I am yours," I don't have to doubt my worth or wonder about the answers to these questions. That phrase, "I am yours," reminds me that God is my heavenly *father,* and what father would give his son or daughter a stone? Not mine—and not yours!

When you do cry out to God, cry out with the attitude that "I am yours."

We all ask questions, and the world will readily throw false answers at us, so we need to be careful to always get our answers from the truth of scripture! Who are you? You are His beloved daughter. That is the correct and final answer.

- Your self-worth is no longer in question!
- Your value is no longer in question!
- Your importance is no longer in question!

Decide to live loved by God, for that is who you truly are. Nothing else matters. His love for you makes you priceless!

> *"Being the beloved is our identity, the core of our existence.*
> *It is not merely a lofty thought, an inspiring*
> *idea, or one name among many.*
> *It is the name by which God knows us*
> *and the way He relates to us."*
> ~ BRENNAN MANNING

BE FEARLESS: *when our identity is correctly defined, there is no going back. Why would we? He has adopted us as His precious children, and He wants us to bring our prayers to Him. So yes, cry out to Him. You are His beloved daughter!*

LET IT SOAK IN

*"Therefore my heart is glad and my tongue
rejoices; my body also will rest secure,"*
~ PSALM 16:9 (NIV)

Daily Meditation: Psalm 16, Joshua 1:6–9

Sometimes I know something in my head, but I don't yet believe it in my heart. You,
too? It's funny, but it can take years for head revelation to take root
in my heart.

Like David, "my heart is glad and my tongue rejoices" when my
head and my heart are working in tandem. When this synchroni-
zation is happening consistently, our bodies "also will rest secure."

To bring our heart to the place where it rests secure, God's word
needs to soak through us from our head to our heart. That sounds
pretty simple and straightforward, but at times it seems to happen
SO slowly! How do we help this process along? I find that the transition occurs in prayer. When I lay my heart before God in times of
prayer, He brings me gladness, rejoicing, and security.

And when I'm on my knees, opening my mind and my heart to
hear His voice, somehow He brings revelation, peace, and all things
good. My job is to let His word soak in, spend time with Him in

prayer, and let His Spirit do the rest. Meditating on His word day and night will bring peace.

Whatever you are seeking to know in your heart will become clearer as you spend time soaking in His presence.

> *"Keep your head and heart going in the right direction,*
> *and you won't have to worry about your feet."*
> ~ AUTHOR UNKNOWN

BE FEARLESS: *I feel like I have so much to learn from God. I know growing in Him is a process, but I am hungry for more. I need him so much! The closer we are to God the more soaking takes place, so let's go ahead and scoot over even closer to Him.*

BUILD YOUR OWN CASTLE

"The wise woman builds her house, but with her own hands the foolish one tears hers down."

~ PROVERBS 14:1 (NIV)

Daily Meditation: Proverbs 14:1, Psalm 127

Kids have an intrinsic and endless drive to create and build. If you've seen them play with blocks, you know what I mean. They try so hard to build great castles and high towers, and then inevitably they make one wrong move and the whole thing comes tumbling down. But in a moment they're back at it, building again.

I think that's the way God meant it to be. He has placed within us a passion to build, to create, to nurture, and to plan. That is what I believe the "wise woman" who "builds her house" is all about. We need to devote ourselves to building with excellence in whatever area God has directed us. Whether that is a family, a career, and/or a ministry, we need to seek to build with wisdom and grace.

God has placed desires within your heart. So go ahead build that castle, and don't become discouraged when the pieces fall. Let God guide you and steady your hands so that you're not working alone; let Him work through you. Even though our "castles" may seem to be tumbling down, with God's help we can build higher than we've ever dreamed!

> "God's plans for my future are far greater than my fears."
> ~ HELEN FAGAN

BE FEARLESS: *it's been said that we are the architects of our own destiny. I think building castles comes naturally because it is part of who we are. Our master builder will help us follow His plan. So keep building, and don't let anyone knock your work (or you!) down.*

NOT A DIY PROJECT

"The one who sent me is with me; he has not left
me alone, for I always do what pleases him."
~ JOHN 8:29 (NIV)

Daily Meditation: John 8:21–30, Hebrews 10:19–25

Today's world is all about DIY—Do It Yourself. Just dive right in and accomplish
whatever it is, all on your own! In your living room? Sure! But in
your life? With your heart? In your life's work? Definitely not.
Instead, we need more of God's presence, more true fellowship
with other believers, and less of doing life "ourselves." As we work
to grow our relationship with God, we have the opportunity to join
in with what He is already doing. Like Jesus, we can declare, "The
one who sent me is with me; he has not left me alone." I don't want
to be alone. I love doing life with God, family, and many friends.
Why would we want to go it alone? It's so much more fun when we
can share life with others along the way!

I'm not talking about whether or not we are married, or have
children, or go to a huge church. I'm talking about a heart revelation that connects us to God's bigger plans for our lives. We are not
alone. We are His. Each one of us always has an audience of One.
Whenever we face a difficult situation in life, we can take comfort
in the fact that God is always with us. Rather than isolating yourself,

seek out fellow believers who will gather around you and support you. The community of God is an incredible thing. Do It Yourself? No, let's Do It Together!

> "Entrepreneurs have a natural inclination to go it alone.
> While this do-it-yourself spirit can help you move forward,
> adding an element of collaboration into the
> mix can make you unstoppable."
> ~ LEAH BUSQUE

BE FEARLESS: *I don't have to prove anything to anyone, and neither do you. Let's do this together! The fact is that you are never really doing anything "DIY" because He is always with you.*

IN PERFECT PEACE

*"You will keep him in perfect peace whose mind
is stayed on You, because he trusts in You."*
~ ISAIAH 26:3 (NIV)

Daily Meditation: Isaiah 26, John 14:25–31

How long has it been since you've truly been at peace? I don't know about you, but sometimes it feels like everywhere I turn, something or someone is clamoring for my attention, and frankly, that can be incredibly overwhelming. Sometimes I feel like I'm stretched so thin that if I get pulled in any more directions, I'll tear right in half! Have you ever felt that way—that there's too much to do, too many people to please, too many stresses and obligations? With so much out there vying for our attention, it can be easy to let our minds dwell on our ever-growing to-do lists. In the midst of all of that chaos, how on earth is it possible to have even a moment of peace?

It all comes down to what we allow our minds to focus on. It's easy to let ourselves get distracted by the chaos of life. So when there's so much to do, how do we keep ourselves from getting over-whelmed? How do we find that "perfect peace" Isaiah talks about? By fixing our minds on God. It's that simple. Just keep your eyes focused on God, your mind fixed on Him, and your heart surrendered to the One who holds the universe in His hand.

Our Father is never overwhelmed by chaos and stress. He is constantly in control of everything, including your life. So fix your mind on Him. Allow Him to fill you with His perfect peace. The struggles and stresses of life will still exist, but if we focus our eyes on Him, everything else will fade into the background. Isaiah goes on to say in 26:4 (NKJV) that in the Lord is "everlasting strength." What an amazing concept! Just trust Him, focus on Him, and He'll give you peace.

> *"He predestined us to adoption as sons*
> *through Jesus Christ to Himself,*
> *according to the kind intention of His will,"*
> ~ EPHESIANS 1:5 (NASB)

BE FEARLESS: *do you want to experience peace in the middle of life's craziness? Then turn your eyes to Jesus. Be intentional about focusing your mind on God. Pray constantly as you go through your day. Trust in God; He will be your strength. And when your mind is stayed on your heavenly Father, you will sense that perfect peace of God that passes all understanding. What a beautiful gift!*

THE LITTLE THINGS

"Indeed, the very hairs of your head are all numbered.
Don't be afraid; you are worth more than many sparrows."
~ LUKE 12:7 (NIV)

Daily Meditation: Luke 12:22–32, Psalm 23

God always takes care of us, even in the little things. You've seen it. I've seen it. And I used to wonder why He cared. Why would God who made the universe be concerned about the little things in our lives that we could really pretty easily get along without?

- It's been a gloomy day ... and he paints the sky with a beautiful sunset.
- We desperately need nice weather for an outdoor event ... and the rain holds off.
- The only parking spot at the dark mall ... is right under the lamp.
- We are feeling down ... and we hear our phone chirp; a friend texts us the exact words we need to read.

Scripture makes it plain that "the very hairs of your head are all numbered." I believe the reason God cares about the little things is because we care about them. If it's important to us, it's important to Him; not as a sign that we are in control, but rather as a sign that He is. I am constantly in awe.

> *"No matter how busy you are, you must take time*
> *to make the other person feel important."*
> ~ MARY KAY ASH

BE FEARLESS: *the fact that the eternal God cares about little me and my little concerns makes me realize afresh and anew just how big He really is! Why He cares is beyond me, but thank goodness He does! With a smile on your face you can face tomorrow, seeing how faithfully your big Father meets your little needs.*

MORE THAN YOU CAN COUNT

"How precious to me are your thoughts, God!
How vast is the sum of them!
Were I to count them, they would
outnumber the grains of sand—
when I awake, I am still with you."
~ PSALM 139:17–18

Daily Meditation: Psalm 139, Psalm 100:3

Have you ever read a verse that makes you say, "Hmm, now that's really good?" I'm sure you know what I mean, a verse or passage that makes you pause and consider something new. Aren't those moments just great? Psalm 139 is full of those moments for me. When I read it, I keep thinking, *Wow, God!*

We know that God fashioned each one of us in our mother's womb. He knows us intimately, and He loves us beyond measure. Now let these words of the psalmist make you pause and consider: "How precious to me are your thoughts ... how vast is the sum of them ... were I to count them they would outnumber the grains of sand."

Isn't that incredible? God's love for you, for me, for every single one of us, is endless. And He is constantly thinking innumerable thoughts about you—more thoughts than there are grains of sand on the planet! That's a lot of love for you.

Let that sink in. Let it wash over your heart and mind. Let it wash away that layer of confusion and doubt. It's simply more than any of us can count!

> *"How do I love thee? Let me count the ways."*
> ~ Elizabeth Barrett Browning

BE FEARLESS: *no matter how hard we try, we truly cannot count the many ways God expresses His love to us. Why He thinks of us so continuously and shows us such amazing love I simply can't fathom. He has more loving thoughts about us than we can count. Laugh and enjoy that new reality!*

PUT AWAY CHILDISH THINGS

*"When I was a child, I talked like a child, I
thought like a child, I reasoned like a child.
When I became a man, I put the ways of childhood behind me."*
~ 1 CORINTHIANS 13:11 (NIV)

Daily Meditation: 1 Corinthians 13:11–12, Ephesians 3:14–21

I loved every phase of watching my children, Megan and Zach, grow up: their first smiles, sleeping through the night, getting out of diapers, losing all their teeth, making their own lunches, doing their own laundry, getting out of braces, driving to college, and finally, leaving the house. Maybe you have witnessed some of these important milestones as well.

Each new day brings its own beauty, and sometimes I long for those childhood days again . . . but we all must grow up. Without a doubt, I know our heavenly Father also enjoys watching us grow up. As we do, He also calls us to grow in Him, to search out His truths, and to dig more deeply into them. This is what it means to put "the ways of childhood behind" us.

And once we're grown, although we may experience some nostalgic moments, we really don't want to go back to being a child.

We'd be reluctant to give up the maturity that comes with age. After all, we worked hard for it! We didn't jump straight from drinking formula to receiving a college diploma, because God has designed growth and maturity to take time. Similarly, we can't jump straight from being a newborn Christian to being a mature believer who knows all the theological answers; that is what the growth process is for. We can continually seek to learn more about God's love and His character each and every day.

As you grow, you can be sure of this: God is proud of you, He celebrates your milestones, and He studies along with you every second of every day. The journey with Him lasts forever!

> *"Learning never exhausts the mind."*
> ~ LEONARDO DA VINCI

———————

BE FEARLESS: *let's gladly throw down our bottles of formula! If the Lord is taking you deeper with Him, jump in! I want to grow and mature in God, don't you? As He helps us, feeds us, and leads us, I will follow. Will you? We are the ones who gain by knowing and growing in Him. And He is walking with us every step of the way.*

NO SHAME HERE

"No one who hopes in you will ever be put to shame,
but shame will come on those who are treacherous without cause."

~ PSALM 25:3 (NIV)

Daily Meditation: Psalm 25, Romans 5:1–10

I don't know about you, but I feel like I have vulnerable moments all the time. As a speaker for women's conferences, I have been known to say something more "real" than "polished" or be overcome with emotion in front of thousands of women. With two kids that I love more than life, I have also been known to be very protective even to the point of occasionally embarrassing my kids! I wish it weren't so, but embarrassment is often inevitable in life.

Shame, on the other hand, is not inevitable. Too many of us have accepted shame as part of our identity. We dwell on the negative things we've experienced, the mistreatment we've endured, or the areas where we believe we've failed, and we forget that God has made us new. When shame tries to tell us we're nothing more than our worst moments, and when fear clouds our minds with doubts, we need to recognize that we're believing a lie—a lie about who God is and who we are. And once we identify the source of that lie (hint: he's our adversary!), we can acknowledge it, refute it, and replace it with the truth about God's unconditional love.

As Psalm 25:3 says, if we believe in the Lord and our hope is in Him, we never need to feel ashamed. God also goes one step further, as He usually does, and comforts us with His promise to "wipe away the tears from all faces" (Isaiah 25:8). Instead of wallowing in shame, we can relax in the comforting presence of God. I love that!

So the next time you experience embarrassment, judgment, criticism, or fear and you're tempted to live in shame, take a breath and choose to let God's amazing love crowd out the shame. Don't let shame get in the way of your freedom and joy in Christ!

> *"Grace means that all of your mistakes now serve*
> *a purpose instead of serving shame."*
> ~ MIKE RUSCH

BE FEARLESS: *you know the end of the story, and shame has no part in it. So fight against shame, say goodbye to it, and replace it with the truth of God's word. Seek out scriptures, songs, and people who remind you of who you really are created to be: a woman full of God's strength, peace, and grace—not Satan's shame!*

YOU GET TO CHANGE

"From that time on Jesus began to preach, 'Repent,
for the kingdom of heaven has come near.'"
~ MATTHEW 4:17 (NIV)

Daily Meditation: 2 Chronicles 32: 24–33, Matthew 4:12–17

Repentance isn't always thought of in a positive light. That's probably because when we repent we are acknowledging that we've done something wrong, and that just doesn't feel good or come naturally to any of us. Nobody wants to admit that they were wrong! Knowing we need to repent can be accompanied by feelings of heaviness, self-doubt, and even sorrow—feelings we really don't want to feel.

When Jesus began his ministry on earth, He started by preaching, "Repent, for the kingdom of heaven has come near." Although we sometimes don't see it this way, His message of repentance was actually one of joy and life, not of condemnation and sadness. His message was an opportunity to walk free, to be whole, and to have a relationship with our Father in heaven. It was an open invitation to turn around, change, and run to the Father no matter how wrong or stubborn we have been. True, godly repentance doesn't stop with a focus backward on our sin; it also draws us forward to

God's healing and restoring grace. This kind of repentance brings us joy and gratitude and renews our desire to please the One who loves us most of all.

I was reflecting on this passage and it hit me: what if we looked at repentance as just that, the chance to change? Then it becomes a positive opportunity presented to us, a call to freedom—and we all want that.

So the next time we need to repent, let's look at it as an opportunity—an opportunity to change.

> *"Repentance, not proper behavior or even*
> *holiness, is the doorway to grace."*
> ~ PHILIP YANCEY

BE FEARLESS: *unlike mere regret, godly repentance always brings freedom. Our pride may not want to admit that we need to repent, but once we do, such a burden is lifted off our shoulders! We should make it a habit to get there—and get freer—faster.*

WALKING IN THE TRUTH

"Now the serpent was more crafty than any of
the wild animals the Lord God had made.
He said to the woman, 'Did God really say, "You
must not eat from any tree in the garden?"' "
~ Genesis 3:1 (NIV)

Daily Meditation: Genesis 3, Matthew 4:1–11

Since the beginning of time, the enemy has been twisting God's words so that they don't quite mean what He intended. The enemy began working on Eve by asking, "Did God really say..." and then he twisted God's words until he had deceived her.

Not much has changed. Everywhere you look, what God calls valuable is mocked and ridiculed. Just spend a few minutes watching TV, surfing the internet, or reading the news and you'll see how society has twisted God's design for marriage, sexual purity, parenting, our role as women, truth, and more.

That is no accident. The enemy is still doing what he does best— lying and deceiving. He throws a tiny lie in among the truth, and little by little the lie gets bigger and starts eating away at the truth.

When you are confronted with lies, turn immediately to scripture. God's word will cut through the confusing fog of lies that the world throws our way. Eve got it right in her first reply when she said, "God did say. . ." (vs. 3a). That is now our job, for the truth is the truth, and it is the truth for a reason: because it brings life and sets us free!

> "Satan gives Adam an apple and takes away
> Paradise. Therefore in all temptations
> let us consider not what he offers, but what we shall lose."
> ~ RICHARD SIBBES

BE FEARLESS: *the next time you sense you are being tempted, take a step back for a moment and look at the situation. Can you identify a lie the enemy is trying to get you to believe? If so, acknowledge it and then walk forward, making a commitment to God and to yourself not to believe or act on the lie.*

WHERE PASSION
GETS ITS FUEL

"for zeal for your house consumes me, and the
insults of those who insult you fall on me."
~ PSALM 69:9 (NIV)

Daily Meditation: Psalm 69, Romans 12:9–21

*I love seeing women who are really in love with Jesus, the ones who are very obvi-*ously passionate about Him and His purposes. They radiate Christ, and spending time in their presence is challenging in a wonderful and refreshing way.

Early on in my journey, such exuberant passion made me wonder, *Where does such wholehearted devotion come from? And is it possible for me to feel that way too?* Have you ever asked yourself the same thing? Where or how do we develop a zeal for the things of God? How do we culti-vate a consuming passion for the Lord?

Passion that is based only on emotion will eventually fizzle out. I have learned that true, enduring passion is fueled by God's word, which is always red-hot and burning. Yes, emotions are great, and so are those emotional highs that can accompany times of great enthusiasm and excitement for the Lord and His purposes. However, enduring desire for God can only be supported by what we know to be true. True passion is fueled by spending time with Him and in His word.

> *"A passion for God isn't necessarily the same as abiding in God; it must be coupled with obedience to be true love for God."*
>
> ~ ED COLE

BE FEARLESS: *we are passionate beings. God has made us that way! Today, make the decision to be passionate about Him Then fuel your passion by consuming His word and spending time with Him.*

WHOM CAN I TRUST?

*"God is not human, that he should lie, not a human
being, that he should change his mind.
Does he speak and then not act? Does he promise and not fulfill?"*
~ NUMBERS 23:19 (NIV)

Daily Meditation: Numbers 23, John 8:21–30

I've discovered that some of those speedy oil-change shops offer special deals on certain days. And while I do appreciate the opportunity to save money, sometimes I've asked myself, *Can I really trust them with my car?* I usually decide that I probably can; it is, after all, just oil, and it's just my car. Sure I want it done right, and although I might do an online rating check, I am not going to do a background check on each of their mechanics.

On the other hand, if I were interviewing a potential babysitter or personal trainer for my kids, then I'd certainly want to know more about the person. They may offer three references, but I'll be looking for ten! That's because feeling safe is essential in any healthy relationship, and trustworthiness must be proven. When it's someone or something we really care about, we want to be sure that we can trust the person.

It would be nice to be able to place absolute trust in people, but the reality is that as humans, we will ultimately fail each other,

disappoint one another, and at times even demonstrate that we are untrustworthy. But imagine if you met someone who never lied or changed their mind, never failed to act, and *always* did what they promised without exception. That person would have earned your trust, and then some! Those characteristics define our Father in heaven. How could you not trust someone like that?

> *"When we trust God more than our feelings, it confuses the devil.*
> *I mean, when he throws you his best shot and*
> *he can't budge you from believing God,*
> *he won't know what to do with you anymore."*
>
> ~ JOYCE MEYER

———————

BE FEARLESS: *make the choice to trust Him. That's a great place to start. Trust has a way of growing when we water it.*

DREAM WEAVER

"Commit your works to the Lord and
your plans will be established."
~ PROVERBS 16:3 (NASB)

Daily Meditation: Psalm 37, Proverbs 16

As a girl, I loved to play house and dream of what my life would be like one day. And now, as a grown woman, I still love to dream . . . about our family's ministry, my children's futures, and places I'd like to visit with my husband.

Dreams are powerful. I believe that the dreams and goals God puts in our hearts inspire us to do His will. However, we must be careful not to confuse our human desires with the divine desires God has given us. Not every dream comes from God! So how do we make the distinction between our selfish, human dreams and our God-given dreams?

Psalm 37:4 (NASB) says, "Delight yourself in the Lord, and He will give you the desires of your heart." I don't think this verse is saying that if you're happy in the Lord, He'll give you whatever you want. Rather, I believe it is saying that as we find our contentment and joy in Him, He will fill our hearts with His dreams that then become our own. Those are the dreams I want to have!

If dreams He has placed in your heart have been shattered by past experiences, it's time to let God restore them. If godly dreams have been sanded away by negative words or attitudes, it's time to let God replace them. If you have traded your God-given dreams for empty, worldly dreams, it's time to ask God to fill your heart with His dreams again.

> "Do not lose hold of your dreams or aspirations.
> For if you do, you may still exist but you have ceased to live."
> ~ HENRY DAVID THOREAU

BE FEARLESS: *dreaming is not only a part of life, it brings life! Our enemy is a thief, so it's no wonder your dreams are sometimes stolen from you, but rest assured: the giver of your dreams, the Lord, is also your biggest supporter!*

YOU ARE MORE THAN ENOUGH

"No, in all these things we are more than
conquerors through him who loved us."
~ ROMANS 8:37 (NIV)

Daily Meditation: Daniel 10, Romans 3:21–31, 8:18–39

Women are attacked with lies about "being enough." At times we are tempted to think that we are enough all on our own merit. We're strong enough, or smart enough, or pretty enough, or talented enough—maybe even more than the women around us. Women who fall prey to this lie start to assume that they parent better than the average mom, are a better friend or employee than most women, and certainly put in more effort than the average gal. This type of self-centered thinking opens the door to pride, judgment, and ultimately isolation.

Another lie is that we can never be enough. Women who internalize this lie believe that others have it more together and have more intrinsic value; that other women are prettier, or funnier, or luckier, and that they will never quite measure up. Being on the losing end of such comparisons doesn't seem fair; it feels shameful and it hurts. Sometimes women facing this lie turn to a relationship or addiction to numb the pain.

Romans 3:23 (NIV) says, "For all have sinned and fall short of the glory of God." Every one of us falls short of what God requires of us no matter how together our lives might seem to be. And yet, because of our identity in Him, every single one of us really IS enough. We are daughters of the King. Our lives are filled to the brim with value, purpose, and fulfillment. We are enough because of who we are in Him.

We actually go from not enough to something way beyond victory. Only God can make that a reality in our lives, a truth that translates directly into hope, joy, peace, rest, strength, grace, wisdom—whatever you need—and even more, because He is in you. Our God is the God of more than enough.

> "Any victory that does not more than conquer
> is just an imitation victory.
> While we are suppressing and wrestling,
> we are only imitating victory.
> If Christ lives in us, we will rejoice in everything,
> and we will thank and praise the Lord.
> We will say, 'Hallelujah! Praise the Lord' forever."
> ~ WATCHMAN NEE

BE FEARLESS: *there is no doubt that I am a conqueror, but not on my own. I am only—and undeniably—a conqueror in the power of Christ. I choose to believe I am who God has already described me to be. He is within me!*

SEEDS TO BE PLANTED

"Therefore encourage one another and build each other up,
just as in fact you are doing."
~ 1 Thessalonians 5:11 (NIV)

Daily Meditation: 1 Thessalonians 5, 1 Peter 4

Growing up in Montana, I helped my mother plant a flower garden each spring. I still love the smell of soil being tilled up—rich, dark clumps of dirt that may seem rather ordinary but make a perfect canvas for dashing tulips and elegant roses.

Psalm 16:5–6 (NKJV) states, "O Lord, You are the portion of my inheritance and my cup; You maintain my lot. The lines have fallen to me in pleasant places; Yes, I have a good inheritance." These verses bring me such peace. It's as if the Lord has assigned to each of us a garden or specific "lot" of land. And inside the garden of life that He has given you there are certain people, some of whom may be especially weary or disheartened, for whom God has given you personal responsibility.

The desire for encouragement is woven through our very being. I need it. You need it. We all need it. Our heavenly Father who designed us to desire relationships lovingly provided avenues to have those needs met. God challenges us to "encourage one another and build each other up."

Take a minute to examine the "lot" God has given you. Do not overwhelm yourself by assuming responsibility for meeting the needs of every weary soul. Instead, choose to rest, knowing that you are only expected to encourage, nourish, and tend to those whom God has specifically assigned to you. Your husband, children, extended family, and friends may come to mind, but also ask the Lord to highlight other individuals who are in your sphere of influence. Maybe it's another mom in the neighborhood or that coworker two cubicles away.

My dear sister, I urge you to plant seeds of encouragement deep into the lives of others by being intentional (do it on purpose), specific (give examples), creative (make it fun), and persistent (do it often). Make someone feel special today. See what happens. You'll never have to take it back. Some things are best when you give them away. Seeds of encouragement are like that. As Tim's dad would always say:

> *"Being kind is one thing you never have to take back."*
> ~ JAMES E. CLINTON

BE FEARLESS: *encouraging words are twice as potent because they have a second harvest. The first harvest is in the lives of the people you impact, and the second harvest is in your own life. Today, ask our heavenly Father to equip you to help other people grow. Planting seeds of encouragement is one of the most enjoyable things we get to do. Sow those seeds!*

TRUSTING AND BEING TRUSTED

"A gossip betrays a confidence, but a trustworthy person keeps a secret."
~ PROVERBS 11:13 (NIV)

Daily Meditation: Proverbs 11, Revelation 21:1–8

Have you ever been betrayed? Have you ever shared with someone something so personal that if others were to find out, it would humiliate you or wound you deeply? We've probably all confided in someone, believing that we could trust them with our "stuff," only to later learn that they had betrayed us.

Having been betrayed makes us extremely afraid to trust and be vulnerable again. It's unfortunately true that while all relationships require a certain level of trust, some obviously require more than others. The relationship you have with your best friend will certainly need to involve a higher level of trust than your relationship with your supervisor at work. And the kind of trust between you and your doctor will look very different from the kind of trust between you and your Pilates instructor.

What may be less obvious, though, is that trustworthiness starts with you. Since you know how much it hurts to be betrayed by someone you trust, doesn't that motivate you to be that much more trustworthy for someone else? Be the kind of person whom others can look to and confide in with confidence.

Thankfully, no matter how many times our trust has been broken and no matter how many times we ourselves have betrayed others, God has *never* broken or betrayed our trust ... and He never will. You can trust Him and go to Him with whatever's on your heart. He is safe, and He is the ultimate example of trustworthiness.

> *"The most important lesson that I have learned*
> *is to trust God in every circumstance.*
> *Lots of times we go through different trials*
> *and following God's plan seems like it*
> *doesn't make any sense at all. God is always*
> *in control and he will never leave us."*
> ~ ALLYSON FELIX

BE FEARLESS: *being a trusting and trustworthy woman is a lofty goal, but it is one you can attain. As you live this way, an amazing thing happens—you attract others just like yourself, thereby surrounding yourself with more and more people who are trustworthy. And together, you can know you serve a trustworthy God!*

FAVOR, NOT FAVORITES

*"Then Peter began to speak: 'I now realize how
true it is that God does not show favoritism
but accepts from every nation the one who
fears him and does what is right.'"*
~ ACTS 10:34–35 (NIV)

Daily Meditation: Psalm 30, Acts 10

Think for a minute about some of your favorite things: your favorite food, your
favorite show, your favorite outfit, your favorite hobby. We all have
things in life that we just enjoy. We may even have a few people
whom we like more than others. We tend to gravitate toward
people who are kind, compassionate, loyal, and selfless. It's hard
not to have a few favorite people in your life whom you are drawn
to more than others.

But God isn't like that. He "does not show favoritism." We are
all incredibly and equally special to Him. Even when we disobey
and let our sin natures get the best of us, He does not love us any
less. He never picks favorites, and nothing we do can ever diminish

His all-consuming love for us. He loves each one of us individually, and we are all complete in Him. There is no favoritism with our Father.

Yet at the same time, He does show us His favor by lavishing His love on each and every one of us! Just take a minute to think about the fact that, as Psalm 30:5 (NIV) says, "His favor lasts a lifetime...." God favors *me*? Yep. And He does so throughout your entire life. Wow.

What does this mean for us? It means that we can rejoice in God's favor! It also means that we need to show favor to the people around us, recognizing that they are all loved by God just as much as we are. Maybe it's that person who just rubs you the wrong way. Maybe it's that person you're harboring a grudge against. Let's follow God's example today and show love to everyone!

> *"God has no favorite children."*
> ~ DAVID YONGGI CHO

———————

BE FEARLESS: *we are His, and that is enough. He welcomes us, period. You are favored by Him, and nothing you can do will change that fact!*

MAKE IT, AND MAKE IT GOOD!

"Yet you, Lord, are our Father. We are
the clay, you are the potter;
we are all the work of your hand."
~ ISAIAH 64:8 (NIV)

Daily Meditation: Isaiah 64, Romans 9:6–29

Remember the sculpture you made out of clay in elementary school—or helped your children make? Our son, Zach, made me a ring holder. It's pretty rough looking, but it is a keepsake I still treasure simply because my boy made it for me.

When it comes to God, the words of Isaiah are so true: "We are the clay, you are the potter." God is at work in your life and my life, smoothing out our rough edges and shaping our core being. Sometimes the process is painful. It hurts to have our rough edges sanded down and be stretched and molded in ways that are new and unfamiliar. But the end result will be far better if we allow God to have free rein in our lives instead of fighting Him every step of the way. I am reminded of the lyrics of the old hymn, "Mold me and make me after Thy will."

This short life is our chance to be something amazing for Him and to let Him craft us into whatever brings Him glory. I say our attitude should be one that boldly submits to the sculptor and declares, "Since you are going to make it, make it good! Don't hold back. I am the work of your hand."

We are clay in the hands of the Master, a master who only has the ability to make beautiful things. The sculpting process may be painful, but the end result will be more wonderful than we can imagine!

> "We are so busy working on God, we
> forget He is trying to work on us.
> That is what this life is all about: God at work on
> us, trying to remake us into vessels of glory."
> ~ DAVID WILKERSON

BE FEARLESS: *nobody said the squishing, pounding, and folding would be fun or easy, but it's the end result that is most appealing. Amazing things happen when we stop trying to mold ourselves and we let the creative Creator take control.*

MASKS

*"You know we never used flattery, nor did we put on
a mask to cover up greed—God is our witness."*
~ 1 Thessalonians 2:5 (NIV)

Daily Meditation: Psalm 15, 1 Thessalonians 2:1–16

Every once in a while we see pictures of celebrities without their makeup on. They look like normal people, and they might even have a blemish or two on their skin!

Seeing these images is a stark reminder of how much we hide about ourselves, literally and figuratively. It also challenges me to wonder how many times we "put on a mask to cover up" parts about us that we think aren't very flattering. These could be personality quirks, physical imperfections or difficulties, or pain we still carry from our past.

But at least we know that everyone takes their masks off at church, right? If only! Unfortunately, all too often women in the church wear a mask that says, "I've got it all together." We want to appear strong and spiritual and perfect. We want to be the model of a "perfect Christian woman" with the "perfect Christian family." So we hide our flaws and imperfections behind a carefully constructed façade, but we aren't fooling God in the slightest. Are we fooling others? Are we fooling ourselves?

Maybe. But we're also doing others—and ourselves—a disservice, because when we wear masks we are essentially lying, and when we lie we lose opportunities to genuinely connect and grow. The reality is that *nobody* has it all together, so trying to live like we do is just not sustainable: we'll eventually break down. Why even let yourself get to that point? Take time to think about what is under your mask: maybe fear, insecurity, or perfectionism. Then prayerfully seek out some safe, godly people with whom you can share your hopes and fears . . . and your secrets mask-free. The rewards will far outweigh the risks.

> *"I'd rather be honest and authentic and disappoint some people*
> *than to exhaust myself trying to keep up the façade of perfection."*
> ~ CRYSTAL PAINE

BE FEARLESS: *living without masks means you are living in freedom. You have the ability—and the choice—to be authentic, bold, and whole. Who doesn't want to live that way?*

DON'T GET CAUGHT

*"Fear of man will prove to be a snare, but
whoever trusts in the Lord is kept safe."*
~ PROVERBS 29:25 (NIV)

Daily Meditation: Proverbs 29, Galatians 1:6–10

My husband, Tim, is a hunter. He loves to go out into the Pennsylvania wilderness and wait for hours for the right animal to pass by. Sometimes he sets traps for the animals so that he can ... well, you know the rest.

Certain parts of our lives can look a lot like these traps—or snares, as some translations call them in Proverbs 29:25. One thing God identifies as a trap is the "fear of man," which basically means being overly concerned with pleasing others and what they might think of us.

We usually ease into the fear of man slowly. The peer pressure, the choices, the beliefs; they can seem good at first. But sooner than we realize it, the trap engages and we are caught. Then we have a hard time getting ourselves free.

On the other hand, if we choose to trust the Lord and care more about His opinion of us than what others think, He promises that we will be safe. We won't get caught in any of these traps. After all, why does it matter what other people think about us? We know how God views us: as His beloved daughters, beautiful and righteous in His eyes because we are redeemed by Jesus Christ. Don't let yourself get caught in the snares of the world. Keep your eyes on Christ and let Him set you free!

> "Until we care more about what God thinks than
> what other people think we are never truly free."
> ~ CHRISTINE CAINE

BE FEARLESS: *we have two choices in life when it comes to the approval we seek. We can either care most about what others think or care most about what our heavenly Father thinks. One brings pain and difficulty, the other brings freedom and life, and we are free to choose whichever we'd like. I know what I'm choosing. What about you?*

DO I GET A DO-OVER?

*"God does all these things to a person— twice, even
three times—to turn them back from the pit, that
the light of life may shine on them."*
~ JOB 33:29-30 (NIV)

Daily Meditation: Job 33, 2 Peter 3

The cup of coffee began to tip. I could see it sliding off the corner of the end table, heading straight down toward the white carpet. My muscles tensed, my hands reached out in slow motion to grab it, but the splash was three feet long before I arrived. Oh, HOW I wished I could replay those few seconds or hit a "backspace" button like the one on my computer. But the coffee seeping into the carpet made it terribly clear that there would be no do-over.

Thankfully, the painful reality of not being able to go back and do something over again does not affect our relationship with God. He is patient with us. God's heart is always to "turn them back from the pit(s)" that we often lead ourselves into. After all, isn't that what salvation is? The Lord doesn't want us to live in sin, separated from Him. Through the death of His Son, Jesus, he made a way for us to be in a relationship with Him that gives us not only a chance for a do-over, but an opportunity for a brand-new life.

We get more than a do-over; we get to *start* over! We're human. We mess up. And as hard as we try to be perfect and not make any mistakes, sometimes our sin nature gets in the way. We'll get coffee stains and dirty smudges all over ourselves throughout our lives, but God continually reaches down to us and wipes away the mess, making us clean and new every day! What an amazing God we serve!

> *"If you are God's child, you are no longer bound*
> *to your past or to what you were.*
> *You're a new creature in Jesus Christ."*
> ~ KAY ARTHUR

BE FEARLESS: *the fact that God is patient with us should be one of our constant praises back to him—not just once, but continuously! The best opportunity we've ever been given for a do-over is through Jesus.*

THERE IS NO ONE LIKE HIM

"No one is like you, Lord; you are great, and
your name is mighty in power."
~ JEREMIAH 10:6 (NIV)

Daily Meditation: Jeremiah 10:1–16, Romans 1:18–32

Remember that Sunday school song we used to sing: "He's got the whole world in His hands?" I find there's a lot of truth conveyed in some of the simple songs we teach our children. Our God really is incredible, holding the entire universe in the palm of His hand! No matter what profession we're in, how influential we are, or even how much we've accomplished for His kingdom, we cannot even begin to compare ourselves with God.

"No one is like you, Lord" pretty much says it all. Not a single person on the planet can even come close! And although we sometimes try to conduct our lives as though we are in charge, there is really only one God.

Those with true power must back it up, and God certainly has. He has proven his limitless power through the creation of the universe. His paintbrushes, covered in stardust, are still wet on His easel. The blueprints and designs for every living thing are rolled up and stacked on His shelf. The universe is His canvas, and everything within it is divinely designed by His glorious power.

As if creation isn't evidence enough, He also proved His power through the miraculous life of Jesus, which included countless miracles as well as a humanly impossible resurrection. We cannot even begin to comprehend the scope of God's might and majesty! Over and over again He does what our finite human brains consider to be "impossible," but nothing, no matter how big or how small, is impossible for God!

If we are attentive enough, we also see His power demonstrated in our own lives each and every day. God isn't required to demonstrate who He is or the power He possesses; He doesn't owe us anything. But I am so thankful that He chose to make Himself known to us in all of His glorious splendor.

> *"It is about the greatness of God, not the significance of man.*
> *God made man small and the universe*
> *big to say something about himself."*
> ~ JOHN PIPER

BE FEARLESS: *I like this definition of "humility": humility is being known for who you are, nothing more and nothing less. Let us kneel today in humility and awe before the throne of our all-powerful God. There is truly no one like Him!*

ABOVE YOURSELVES

"Do nothing out of selfish ambition or vain conceit.
Rather, in humility value others above yourselves,"
~ PHILIPPIANS 2:3

Daily Meditation: Philippians 2:1–18, Mark 9:30–37

Have you ever felt like someone is looking right through you? Maybe you're having a conversation with someone and you just sense that the person isn't really hearing you or connecting with you in that moment. I've experienced that. It makes me feel invisible, almost like I don't exist.

Doesn't it hurt to feel that way? In those types of situations—and they definitely take place in many different ways—I have come to the conclusion that there is nothing I can do about the other person or how they're engaging—or not engaging—with me. But I can do something about me.

In Philippians 2, we are encouraged to value others more than we value ourselves. That can be really hard to do, especially when we feel slighted or devalued by someone else. But even then, God's word encourages us to not think about ourselves and our own interests all the time; instead, we should care more about others. You never know what might be going on in their lives that's causing them fear or worry, making them seem distracted and disinterested.

The next time I'm talking with someone and I get the sense that they're just not there with me, I'm going to remember what God tells me to do. I'm going to take a moment to ask them how they are doing and really listen, making sure that in that moment they know that I value them more than myself.

> *"Everybody can be great. Because anybody can*
> *serve. You don't have to have a college degree*
> *to serve. You don't have to make your subject*
> *and your verb agree to serve.*
> *You don't have to know the second theory of*
> *thermodynamics in physics to serve.*
> *You only need a heart full of grace,*
> *a soul generated by love."*
> ~ Dr. Martin Luther King, Jr.

BE FEARLESS: *we are more loved by God than we will ever understand. So is every other person you encounter. Challenge yourself to see them the way God sees them.*

BEING A FRIEND INDEED

"One who has unreliable friends soon comes to ruin,
but there is a friend who sticks closer than a brother"
~ PROVERBS 18:24 (NIV)

Daily Meditation: Proverbs 18, John 15:1–17

Good girlfriends are one of the purest sources of joy and encouragement in life, don't you think? For me, they're the first people I call when something goes wrong, and at this stage of my life, I've even got some of them on speed dial! They're the ones you turn to and lean on when one of your parents gets discouraging news from the doctor, or when you take your two-year-old to the ER with a 105-degree temperature, or when your husband loses his job. Those friends are your rock. We all need friends like that, and we all should also try to be friends like that.

But what about when the everyday, ordinary issues of life come up? Are we still those kinds of friends then? All too often, we miss out on helping with our friends' little things because we aren't even aware they exist. Maybe we are too busy to notice, or maybe those little things are kept a secret. Either way, we miss opportunities to be a true friend.

Be the kind of friend who not only rushes in when the crises of life happen, but who also pays attention and notices the little things in others' lives. Needs are everywhere. Just keep your eyes and heart open and you will find many opportunities to help carry the loads of others.

> "The best of friends to us will always be
> friends who imitate Christ."
> ~ ALISTAIR BEGG

BE FEARLESS: *there is, of course, no end to the needs, but there is an end to the friends who notice. You can't do it all, and that is okay. But you can make a difference.*

HOPE IN GOD

"Why, my soul, are you downcast? Why so disturbed within me?
Put your hope in God, for I will yet praise
him, my Savior and my God. "
~ PSALM 43:5 (NIV)

Daily Meditation: Psalm 43, Romans 5

Everybody gets the blues from time to time. We all have occasional bad days that come and go, but there are also difficult seasons in this life. Sometimes in the midst of a hard time, it seems impossible to believe that "this too shall pass" and we need faith and perseverance to get "unstuck."

King David was no stranger to the burden of painful emotions. He is the psalmist who asked himself, "Why, my soul, are you downcast? Why so disturbed within me?" Have you ever asked yourself the same questions? Perhaps you have wondered, *Why do I feel this way?* or *Why is this so difficult for me?* Be like King David who, after seeking the Lord, followed his questions by commanding his soul to "Put your hope in God" (Psalm 43:5). What an example of resolve!

Right now it may seem like you are pushing through mud, but do not lose heart. Restoration is a process. "Spiritual deliverance or emotional transformation may happen in an instant—but the manifestation of that in routines, habits, and choices of your life is an ongoing process that is intended by God to grow stronger and more profound day by day" (*Bounce Back: When Your Heart Is Empty and Your Dreams Are Lost*, p34). In the meantime, let's train our brains to tell our hearts that if we lose our hope, we need to take a deep breath and press in closer to God, the giver of hope.

When David wrote, "Put your hope in God," the tone of Psalm 43 changed. He immediately started praising God. Friend, if you are reading this devotional today in your own dark season, can I invite you to praise our Father? While praise may not be your first instinct in this moment, take heart. Begin with a favorite worship song or a familiar passage. When we praise God we focus on Him and His greatness, and in so doing, we know exactly where we are: we are in His arms. He will see us through!

> *"Hope means expectancy when things are otherwise hopeless."*
> ~ G. K. CHESTERTON

BE FEARLESS: *choose beforehand to go to the hope giver when you need hope. Focus on seeing Him, trusting Him, and knowing He is there for you. Your Father will plant new seeds of life and hope into your heart. He has massive heaps of hope. You ask; He will give it.*

GUARD YOUR MIND

"Set your mind on things above, not on earthly things."
~ Colossians 3:2 (NIV)

Daily Meditation: Colossians 3, Philippians 4

If I were to write down every task that needs to be accomplished, everything I want to get done, and each need that every person wants me to fulfill, I would spend a day just making that list! In a world where demands seem endless, the key to investing time wisely and being productive in the spaces that matter most is prioritizing I keep a priority list every day to remind myself of what is essential. If I don't, I grow frustrated by the many needs vying for my attention.

The same way we use a priority list to control our daily tasks, we can choose where we'll invest our thoughts We can't ruminate on every idea, concern, or worry that tries to steal our attention. The mind can be a very beautiful, free, creative place . . . or a very dark, confused, turbulent place. Consider the contrast:

- *Happy* . . . or angry thoughts
- *Peaceful* . . . or worrisome thoughts
- *Loving* . . . or hateful thoughts
- *Pure* . . . or lustful thoughts
- *Joyful* . . . or depressed thoughts

- *Giving* ... or selfish thoughts

When scripture challenges us to "set your mind on things above," we can choose where to direct our thoughts. But this doesn't happen automatically! The snakes of bitterness, jealousy, hate, negativity, or self-condemnation can easily enter through vehicles such as social media, television, or even conversations we participate in. Paul encourages us in Philippians 4:8 (NIV), "Finally, brothers and sisters, whatever is true, whatever is noble, whatever is right, whatever is pure, whatever is lovely, whatever is admirable—if anything is excellent or praiseworthy—think about such things." To fulfill this command, we must actively filter what we allow in front of our eyes and into our ears. These decisions must not be dismissed as minute or unimportant. In 2 Corinthians 2:11 scripture refers to the schemes Satan uses to try to outwit us followers of Christ. My sisters, a lack of attention, discipline, or conviction in one area can open a door of vulnerability for the adversary to set up camp in our minds. Let's be on guard and proactive tending to our thoughts.

> *"The battle for sin always starts in the mind."*
> ~ RICK WARREN

BE FEARLESS: *one way to beat distractions is to expect them to pop up, and then be prepared to stick to your priority list. Rely on the Lord's strength to help you do this. Pray over your priorities and the responsibilities He has given you to steward. Distractions will come, but you can overcome them by making a preemptive choice to focus on what the Bible says is true.*

HOW TO GIVE BLESSINGS

*"And God is able to bless you abundantly, so
that in all things at all times,
having all that you need, you will abound in every good work."*
~ 2 Corinthians 9:8 (NIV)

Daily Meditation: Luke 6, Matthew 6

I can't think of a single person who does not like to be blessed. I know I surely do! As Christians, we have the opportunity to give blessings to each other on a daily basis. What do blessings look like? They can be gifts, words of affirmation, praying for one another, or even the act of forgiving. A blessing can come in pretty much any form, based on what the person needs right then and there. It's through showing blessing that we really live out the practical side of love, empathy, and kindness.

We are so blessed! God blesses us each day with good health, shelter, food to eat, friends, and family. God has modeled giving good gifts, and we should seek to follow His example. The Bible talks about striving to be like Christ every single day, and we can live that out through the act of blessing others.

It's worth noting that as explained in 1 Corinthians 13, we are nothing without love. Our heart attitude is at least as important as our outward action, so when we give someone a blessing with a wrong attitude, it is meaningless to them and to God. You can usually tell when someone is doing something without really meaning it; it makes the gift taste bitter. The Lord looks at the heart, and He knows the motivation of our heart when we're giving to someone else.

Deuteronomy 15:10 (NIV) says, "Give generously to them and do so without a grudging heart; then because of this the Lord your God will bless you in all your work and in everything you put your hand to." Giving blessings not only blesses the people we are giving to, it can also bless us in return!

And what is the main reason we bless other people in the first place? Because *we've* been impossibly blessed! God blessed us beyond imagination by sending His one and only son, Jesus Christ, to die for our sins. What an example of sacrificial love!

> *"I believe He wants us to love others so much*
> *that we go to extremes to help them."*
> ~ FRANCIS CHAN

BE FEARLESS: *God has blessed us more than we could ever imagine, so let's be a blessing to others on a daily basis, bringing change and love to the people around us. Today let's make it our mission to bless someone else through the act of giving, prayer, or an encouraging word. Every day we should focus on being a blessing to someone in some way.*

YOUR HEAVENLY FATHER

"And, 'I will be a Father to you, and you will be my
sons and daughters, says the Lord Almighty.' "
~ 2 CORINTHIANS 6:18 (NIV)

Daily Meditation: 2 Corinthians 6:14–18, Psalm 27

There's something special about a little girl's relationship with her father. Watching Tim interact with our daughter, Megan, always brings a smile to my face. Something about that daddy-daughter bond is just so precious!

Perhaps you, too, had a wonderful relationship with your father. What a blessing that is! Yet I know many are not as fortunate and do not have a relationship with their father. Perhaps you grew up in a fatherless home or had a bad relationship with your father for one reason or another. If that is the case, my heart aches for you. But listen, dear sister: God will always be your heavenly Father.

I love the word that God uses to describe himself as our Father, *Abba*. This signifies not just a biological relationship but a close, intimate, loving relationship between a parent and child. That's the kind of relationship God wants to have with you! You're His little girl, His beloved daughter. Wow! What an awesome God we serve!

This can be hard to grasp if you didn't have an ideal relationship with your earthly father, but let me remind you of these truths:

- You are loved.
- You are valuable.
- You have a heavenly Father who will take care of all your needs.
- You are a daughter of the King.

> *"The true measure of God's love is that He loves without measure."*
> ~ AUTHOR UNKNOWN

BE FEARLESS: *God has given us the people in our lives for a reason. Even when that reason is hard to see, we can cling to the hope and promise that our heavenly Father will meet all our needs and will never leave us nor forsake us. He's the best father anyone could ever have!*

THE DESTRUCTIVE TONE

"Mockers resent correction, so they avoid the wise."
~ PROVERBS 15:12 (NIV)

Daily Meditation: James 3, Colossians 3:1–17

It's amazing how the same phrase can mean so many different things depending on how you say it. Tone of voice makes such a difference. For example, words that may seem harmless on the surface can be incredibly cutting when they are spoken harshly or laced with sarcasm.

Destructive communication can be a major problem in our interactions. When we speak mockingly to others, we not only risk destroying our relationship with them, we also cheapen our witness for Christ. What a tragedy.

It is vitally important for us to train ourselves to speak in a way that encourages and edifies the people around us. The words we use affect people more than we know; one negative phrase can stick with a person for the rest of their life! Do you really want the lasting impression you make on someone's life to be a negative one? Let's not be people who inject poison into the lives of others with our words. Instead, let's be known for showing truth and love.

God is always listening. He hears every word that falls from our lips, and He will hold us accountable for every hasty word. In verse after verse, the scriptures describe the power of the tongue and the consequences that can occur when words are allowed to spew out without care. Matthew 12:36 (NASB) states, "But I tell you that every careless word that people speak, they shall give an accounting for it in the day of judgment." Yikes! I'd better watch my mouth!

> *"Your words can permanently influence a life."*
> ~ JERRY FALWELL

————————

BE FEARLESS: *maybe you've been hurt by condescending and painful words, or maybe you've slipped into a habit of speaking negatively to those around you. Either way, watching our own words is so important! Let us make the decision today to speak in love, even when we are upset. God is listening, so let's speak only things that will please Him and bring Him joy.*

GIVING MY ALL TO HIM

"Whatever you do, work heartily, as for the Lord and not for men,
knowing that from the Lord you will receive
the inheritance as your reward.
You are serving the Lord Christ"
~ COLOSSIANS 3:23–24 (ESV)

Daily Meditation: Matthew 16:24, Proverbs 23:26

It's so easy to slip into apathy in the midst of our daily grind. The chores. The kids.
The job. The same routine that just keeps on going day after day after day. When will it ever end?

It will end when your perspective changes! Paul's message in Colossians 3:23–24 is simple: Listen up: whatever you do, do it for God! It doesn't matter what you're doing. You can glorify God through absolutely anything. Whether it's changing diapers, working in your office, or shopping for groceries, you can do everything with the attitude of seeking to please God. And God wants us to move through our days with joy. He smiles upon us when we go through life having fun.

The crazy thing is that every day we have is a gift from God! The items on our to-do list shouldn't be viewed as things we *have* to do, but rather as things we *get* to do! Let's make this fun; let's think about how we can turn ordinary tasks like doing the dishes into times to worship, pray, or dream about fun ways we might bless others in the coming days. Let's make the mundane holy by changing our attitude! Giving our all requires a constant decision to glorify and obey. As 1 Corinthians 10:31 (NIV) reads, "So whether you eat or drink or whatever you do, do it all for the glory of God."

We may be doing boring and ordinary tasks, but if we do them as unto the Lord, it will change our lives!

> *"There will never be enough thanks, never enough*
> *words nor thoughts high or deep enough*
> *to adequately convey His worth. I don't know how*
> *to give back to the Lord what He deserves*
> *other than to just offer Him my life and every part of me."*
> ~ KARI JOBE

———————

BE FEARLESS: *let's devote ourselves today to finding ways to honor and glorify God in the little things. If everything we say and do is done in the name of Jesus to bring Him praise, we can expect God to do the unexpected on our behalf!*

IT'S STILL AMAZING GRACE

"Restore to me the joy of your salvation and
grant me a willing spirit, to sustain me."
~ PSALM 51:12 (NIV)

Daily Meditation: Matthew 11, Psalm 51

What burden are you carrying today? It's time to lay it down. When you hold onto burdens, your shoulders ache from the weight, and your steps are slowed because you are continually weighed down. Your past may be a heavy burden, but you can be freed from that weight! While acknowledging the pain we've endured, when we stand face to face with God's perspective of our past, we really can't respond with anything less than gratefulness and deep appreciation for His grace and mercy in our lives.

God has taken our burdens from us! Do you remember the day when He lifted the burden of sin from your life? The life-changing moment you accepted Christ? When we truly comprehend what Jesus did for us, we either stand amazed or fall flat on our faces, bowing in awe and thankfulness to our holy Father! Either way, we are fully confident that His demonstration of love will forever play a crucial role in our lives.

But then time goes by. Memories fade, and slowly but surely we start picking up our burdens again, forgetting that we no longer have to carry them. But although we may have forgotten the power of that incredible moment, His grace is no less passionate, His mercy is just as powerful, and His love is still as far-reaching now as it was then. The only difference is in our own minds. Our memory may have faded, but the intense glory of his redemption shines as brightly as ever! Maybe that is why the psalmist prayed, "Restore to me the joy of your salvation."

This fading of reality affects all of us, especially second- and third-generation Christians. Life gets in the way and we start taking on worldly burdens again. So how do we stop? The way to fight this tendency is to:

1. Remember and rehearse the many great things God has done for you.
2. Boldly declare (out loud) that your forgetting in no way weakens or minimizes His accomplishments.
3. Continually surrender your burdens to Him and experience His strength in your spirit.

> *"I'd advise you, then, to quickly get rid of your burden;*
> *for until then you'll never be settled in your mind*
> *or enjoy the benefits of the blessings that God has given you."*
> ~ JOHN BUNYAN, *Pilgrim's Progress*

––––––––––

BE FEARLESS: *take action by remembering. Lay your burdens down at Jesus's feet, and remember that you don't need to take them up again! This truth gives you strength and immediately fills your mouth with praise!*

REST ISN'T FOR THE WEAK

"Then, because so many people were coming and going
that they did not even have a chance to eat, he said to them,
'Come with me by yourselves to a quiet place and get some rest.'"
~ MARK 6:31 (NIV)

Daily Meditation: Exodus 33:12–22, Hebrews 4

Being a hard worker is an essential quality that is addressed and commended throughout scripture. God makes it clear that he doesn't tolerate laziness, and He rewards those who work hard. Proverbs 12:24 (NIV) says, "Diligent hands will rule, but laziness ends in forced labor."

But in addition to hard work, God also values taking time to rest in order to remain emotionally, physically, and spiritually healthy. When God created the earth, He took the seventh day to rest. Genesis 2:2–3 (NIV) says, "By the seventh day God had finished the work he had been doing; so on the seventh day he rested from all his work. Then God blessed the seventh day and made it holy, because on it he rested from all the work of creating that he had done."

If God took time to rest, why shouldn't we? We are frequently hard on ourselves and do not give ourselves enough credit for all we have accomplished. Constant busyness can be harmful to our walk with God and to our personal relationships. Taking time to rest and spend time with God is essential and necessary to our spiritual development. Taking time to rest is not a form of weakness, it is a sign of strength and maturity.

> "Rest time is not waste time. It is economy
> to gather fresh strength...
> It is wisdom to take occasional furlough.
> In the long run, we shall do more by sometimes doing less."
> ~ CHARLES SPURGEON

BE FEARLESS: *working hard and also taking time to rest are two key components of developing spiritual maturity. It is vital that we take time out of our busy schedules to rest and regain strength for the journey ahead. Rest is good for our heart and should not be something we look down upon. Rest is for the strong.*

LET ALL MY WORDS BE SWEET

"How sweet are your words to my taste,
sweeter than honey to my mouth!"
~ PSALM 119:103 (NIV)

Daily Meditation: Psalm 119:97–104, Matthew 23

"We don't do that here!" the elderly woman whispered sharply, and the young girl who dared to let her feet move to the rhythm of the song at church slowly crept back to her seat, feeling ashamed and embarrassed.

Words have great power. We all know from personal experience just how powerful—and painful—words can be. But there is one extra ingredient that can really multiply the strength and viciousness of the spoken word: legalism! We add to the scriptures rules and regulations that are not found within its pages and, as a result, we isolate people and push them away from the truth.

Oh, that my words would reflect my Father's heart and be as beneficial as His words, for "sweet are your words to my taste, sweeter than honey to my mouth!" I want people to hear those kinds of words from my mouth and be encouraged and uplifted! But when we sprinkle the spice of legalism over our words, we are spreading bitterness that brings death instead of life.

It's tempting to focus on rules that set clear parameters and keep us from having to evaluate each situation individually, but our focus should be on Jesus. We have a relationship with Him, not with legalistic rules. And what's more, His words are sweet! When we dwell in the presence of our holy God, our words will reflect the company we keep. If we spend time around people who are negative, legalistic, and discouraging, our words will start to reflect those attributes as well. But if we spend our time with Jesus and surround ourselves with people who are encouraging and positive, our words will change, and so will our lives!

> *"We can only offer true healing with our words*
> *when we have a strong spiritual life.*
> *By focusing on our relationship with God,*
> *we're also focused on the source of all wisdom in our lives."*
> ~ LAUREN C. MOYE

BE FEARLESS: *words are powerful. You know that from personal experience. Let's focus on keeping our words pleasant and uplifting. Let's follow God's example and use our words to bless other people, not tear them down.*

LET GO OF THE SNAKE!

"Like a coating of silver dross on earthenware
are fervent lips with an evil heart."
~ PROVERBS 26:23 (NIV)

Daily Meditation: Proverbs 13:20, Matthew 12:33–37

We are relational people; that's just how we are wired. It's in our genes, and it's how we think and communicate. And although we are not stupid, sometimes, when we're not paying close attention, we can overlook subtle tweaks to the truth and, without realizing it, be swayed by false words and backhanded compliments.

I've read things and been told things that sound like the truth, and then later in a moment of quietness, I've realized that, *Hey, that wasn't the truth after all!* This can happen with a doctrine that proves to be unscriptural and also with "friends" who continually drag you down. I love the imagery in Proverbs when it talks about a clay pot covered with silver; at first glance it's shiny and beautiful, but when you look more closely you see that it's nothing but a sham, a false front meant to deceive.

If you have friends in your life who, like snakes, are injecting their venomous fangs into you and trying to poison you with their words, I challenge you: let go of the snake! Enough is enough! This is your life, and you are able to set boundaries. Just because we are committed to love and pray for certain people in our lives doesn't mean we are required to make excuses, ignore bad behavior, or pretend we deserve mistreatment. Speak the truth in love, but by all means don't let people continue to harm you.

> *"False words are not only evil in themselves, but they infect the soul with evil."*
> ~ SOCRATES

BE FEARLESS: *snakes bite; that's what they do. And we need to locate them and move out of their way before they infect us with their venom! Stand up for the truth; don't let others' lies and poison get under your skin. Don't be afraid to stand up for yourself and for the truth. Be wise in choosing your friends, create and maintain healthy boundaries, and be willing to have honest conversations. Then, even if they walk away after you confront them, you are free!*

FINDING OUR APPROVAL

*"Do not be afraid of those who kill the
body but cannot kill the soul.
Rather, be afraid of the One who can
destroy both soul and body in hell."*
~ MATTHEW 10:28 (NIV)

Daily Meditation: Psalm 118:6–9, Matthew 10:26–42

We all seek approval. This desire to be affirmed and accepted is rooted in us from an early age, and whether or not we obtained this approval from our parents, siblings, teachers, or friends, we all still feel the deep longing to be approved by those around us.

The desire for approval is there because we actually *need* approval. God created us that way, so we should not try to pretend that need doesn't exist. Ignoring it won't make it go away, nor will rejecting people, which is how some women cope with their need for approval.

When Jesus said, "Do not be afraid of those who kill the body but cannot kill the soul," He made very clear who the provider of our approval must be: our Father in heaven, and Him alone!

Truly, God's opinion of us is far more important than any human being's opinion.

At the end of the day, the end of the year, or the end of our lives, it is God whom we serve, and it is His approval we seek. He is the one we live for here and now. I want to know that He looks upon my life and smiles at what He sees.

> *"The increased desire to please God and seek HIS approval*
> *will decrease the desire to seek approval from man."*
> ~ YVONNE PIERRE

BE FEARLESS: *although we can feel affirmed when we please other people, realizing that I really only need to seek God's approval is such a freeing reality. Start with that truth in your mind, push it down into your heart, and then live your life accordingly!*

PUT AWAY THE MATCHES

*"A hot-tempered person stirs up conflict, but
the one who is patient calms a quarrel."*
~ PROVERBS 15:18 (NIV)

Daily Meditation: Proverbs 15, James 1:19–20

The anger and hurt were very real. The older sister, hurt by the younger sister, was battling betrayal and disappointment. Then the mother stepped in and made things even worse by ridiculing the older sister. The bridge of relationship between the two sisters was dry, weak, and ready to burn. One match was all it would take. All the past could be burned up in an instant … but rather than igniting the fire, the older sister blew out her own match.

She chose to pray, forgive, and patiently work it out, for "the one who is patient calms a quarrel," and that is precisely what she did. Yes, in the middle of the fight the older sister had every right to set that bridge on fire and watch it burn. She was justified, and her mother had spitefully jumped into the thick of things, slinging lies around like it was a food fight.

But since the older sister made the counterintuitive choice to put away the matches, slowly, bit by bit, things improved. The younger sister grew up and became a mother, and today the two sisters are good friends.

Though it may be very tempting, don't light the bridge on fire. Decide to blow out the match. Patiently, do all you can to spray the dry bridge with water. In time, it will become an amazing architectural wonder that will serve you well.

> *"Patience is not simply the ability to wait—*
> *it's how we behave while we're waiting."*
> ~ JOYCE MEYER

BE FEARLESS: *burning a bridge almost always creates a bigger mess that requires more work later. But with God's help, we can wisely and patiently navigate painful situations. Be strong, be wise, and live in a way that makes Him proud.*

HAVING A PERFECT MEMORY

*"Friend deceives friend, and no one speaks the truth.
They have taught their tongues to lie; they
weary themselves with sinning."*
~ JEREMIAH 9:5 (NIV)

Daily Meditation: Jeremiah 9:1–6, Colossians 3:5–10

Imagine trying to teach someone who is learning English as a second or third language exactly how a lie can be *little* or *white* or *stretched.* It makes no sense at all when you stop and think about it. How can an abstract concept be a size, color, or shape?

This question should confuse all of us! A lie is a lie no matter what it is called. The words "Friend deceives friend" and "They have taught their tongues to lie" are painfully accurate, as are "They weary themselves with sinning."

It was Mark Twain who said, "If you tell the truth, you don't have to remember anything." Having a perfect memory is easy; simply tell the truth. Then there are no stories to make up, no alternative versions to remember, no worry about forgetting incriminating facts, and no fear of being found out.

When we always tell the truth, we will actually be:

- Peaceful!
- Restful!
- Free!
- Joyful!
- Unashamed!

Those qualities are all yours and mine, if we want them. All we have to do is speak the truth. And that makes total sense.

> *"Always tell the truth, and you can tell it the same way every time."*
> ~ WILLIAM MARRION BRANHAM

BE FEARLESS: *lying is such a bad habit. Let us train our lips to speak the truth. Telling the truth cultivates an environment for freedom to take root and thrive!*

THE SECRET TO BEING CONTENT

"I have learned the secret of being content
in any and every situation,
whether well fed or hungry, whether living in plenty or in want."
~ PHILIPPIANS 4:12B (NIV)

Daily Meditation: 2 Corinthians 12:9−10, Philippians 4

I love secrets! What woman doesn't? Although most secrets, by definition, are best left unsaid, some secrets actually should *not* be kept private. They need to be shared, passed around, and often repeated. Such is the secret of contentment.

The apostle Paul is a good example. Now being shipwrecked, beaten, and persecuted is certainly not on my bucket list of things I want to do, but what I do want to master is being content. Paul said, "I have learned the secret of being content in any and every situation." I want to learn that too.

So what is the secret to contentment? Here it is:

1. Keep your eyes on Jesus.
2. Avoid comparison with others at all costs.
3. Never adopt a "victim" mentality.

When we walk in contentment, the world is truly a better place, opportunity abounds, the grass is greener on our side of the fence, we have something wonderful to offer to others, and we are whole. So go ahead and share it; that is one secret you can tell the world!

"Contentment does not mean that I desire nothing.
But rather, it's the simple decision to be happy with what I have."
~ PAULA ROLLO

———————

BE FEARLESS: *contentment is not only a secret, it is my own personal choice. Nobody else can do it for me. Those who live a contented life really are enviable! Be enviable but freely give away your secret.*

I DON'T NEED TO GET IT

*"Such knowledge is too wonderful for
me, too lofty for me to attain."*
~ PSALM 139:6 (NIV)

Daily Meditation: Psalm 131, Psalm 139:1–6

When talking with our friends about deep things, we often hear—and say—things
like, "I just don't get it" and "Why did God do that?" Below the
surface of such a conversation sits a boiling pot that just won't
simmer down, and inside that pot are all the unanswered questions.

For many women, that pot boils over and drama erupts . . . feelings are hurt, unkind words are said, and belief in God weakens.
But over time the eruption cools, and then you might (or might
not) find out what the real problem was.

I learned years ago that I do not need to understand all that
happens to me. The psalmist said it perfectly when he wrote, "Such
knowledge is too wonderful for me, too lofty for me to attain."
When it comes to what God is doing in my life and in the lives of
those around me, I do not need to "get it."

Oh, sure, I *want* to understand, but I do not *need* to understand.
God doesn't have to ask my permission to do anything. I will do my

best to play my part in his divine plans, but truly "getting" all that he is doing is not a requirement. And I'm learning to be okay with that wonderful reality.

> "Where you are today is no accident. God is
> using the situation you are in right now
> to shape you and prepare you for the place He
> wants to bring you into tomorrow.
> Trust Him with His plan even if you don't understand it."
> ~ AUTHOR UNKNOWN

BE FEARLESS: *trusting, not asking why, is my job. But that doesn't mean we don't need to pray for help! Pray without ceasing and trust Him to guide you.*

WHAT TRULY MATTERS

*"What is more, I consider everything a loss
because of the surpassing worth
of knowing Christ Jesus my Lord, for
whose sake I have lost all things.
I consider them garbage, that I may gain
Christ and be found in him,"*
~ PHILIPPIANS 3:8–9A (NIV)

Daily Meditation: Luke 10:38–42, Philippians 3:1–14

When we think of the great heroes of faith in the Bible, one of the people who usually comes to mind is the apostle Paul. He wrote many books of the Bible, lived an amazing life for God, performed incredible miracles, and endured terrible suffering throughout his life. He also had all sorts of worldly credentials to his name, things that defined him as an upperclass citizen of his day. He was clearly a big shot in his community, with power and authority and status, but he gave up all of that.

Paul wrote in his letter to the Philippians—from a prison cell, no less!—that all of his personal achievements and status symbols, all the prestige and accomplishments that had made his life comfortable before meeting Christ, all the things that the world considered impressive, were "garbage" in comparison to knowing Jesus. We're talking smelly trash full of dirty diapers, eggshells, and coffee grounds! The things in life we've done, the status we've gained, the works that we're proud of—all of it useless! Nothing but garbage and waste! What a humbling thought.

When I think about all the things in life I am proud of, I ask myself, *How important are they in comparison to knowing Jesus?* Actually they're not important at all, and that's a perspective I never want to lose. So whether it's praise or persecution, accomplishment or accusation, let's not let anything get in the way of knowing Christ. The most important thing we can do in this life is to devote ourselves to God and invite Him to work through us. What a joy to have a relationship with Christ!

> *"Nothing teaches us about the preciousness of the Creator*
> *as much as when we learn the emptiness of everything else."*
> ~ CHARLES SPURGEON

BE FEARLESS: *nothing this life can throw at us is more important that knowing God! Don't let wealth, status, or accomplishments get in the way of your relationship with Christ, because that's what truly matters.*

KEEP THE HOPE CANDLE BURNING

*"Though he slay me, yet will I hope in him; I
will surely defend my ways to his face."*
~ JOB 13:15 (NIV)

Daily Meditation: Job 13, Romans 1:5–11

*A boxer once said, "All I need to do to win is get up one more time than my
opponent."* To me, that is the epitome of hope. It says, "Sure, I will
get knocked down. I expect that, but know this: I plan to get up one
more time than you do!"

Hope is bold. It is courageous. It is belligerent in the face of
opposition. It is relentless. And it is strong because it is rooted
in two certainties: the past certainty that Jesus died on the cross
to bring us into the family of God, and the future certainty that
someday in the new heaven and new earth, all things will be made
right. Because those truths are our constant source of confidence
and hope, we have what it takes to handle the problems of today.

We can be sure of the hope we have in the Lord, no matter
what difficult circumstances come our way. Job said it best when

he declared, "Though he slay me, yet will I hope in him." That is someone who knows his God!

Hold fast to your hope. Who cares if people think you're naïve or crazy for believing that God has called you for something more than your current situation? It's your choice to maintain your hope.

With you, I am also holding on to hope. I choose to believe that a new day will dawn, that a new opportunity will arise, and that I will see my God be mighty in my situation. As long as I have breath, I am going to believe in Him. That is my reason and source of hope.

> "My hope is built on nothing less
> Than Jesus' blood and righteousness;
> I dare not trust the sweetest frame,
> But wholly lean on Jesus' name.
> On Christ, the solid Rock, I stand;
> All other ground is sinking sand."
> ~ EDWARD MOTE

BE FEARLESS: *no darkness can withstand even the smallest light, so keep your hope candle burning. God is with you this very moment. Your candle is going to start a fire!*

RELAX IN THE MOMENT

*"And we know that in all things God works
for the good of those who love him,
who have been called according to his purpose."*
~ ROMANS 8:28 (NIV)

Daily Meditation: Psalm 29, Romans 8

It is always easier said than done. That's how I feel about any words of comfort offered to me when I'm in the thick of things with pressures, obstacles, and deadlines banging on my door. In that moment, catching my breath and relaxing sounds easier said than done, but the truth is that I still need to do it!

I know that "in all things God works for the good of those who love him, who have been called according to his purpose," but that does not mean it's easy to relax. For most of us, it's rather difficult to relax in stressful situations. In the story of Jesus and the disciples crossing the lake during the raging storm, Jesus was asleep in the bottom of the boat! That's my goal too—to be able to fall asleep in the midst of whatever storm is raging around me, but the only way to sleep in a storm is to know that the outcome is going to be good.

In your own stressful situation you already know the outcome, for God promised to make things work for your good. So go ahead taste the spray, squeeze the water out of your hair, or get another umbrella if you need to ... and then boldly and confidently lie back on your pillow!

> *"In a storm of struggles, I have tried to control the elements,*
> *clasp the fist tight so as to protect self and happiness.*
> *But stress can be an addiction, and worry*
> *can be our lunge for control,*
> *and we forget the answer to this moment*
> *is always yes because of Christ."*
> ~ Ann Voskamp

BE FEARLESS: *in the moment it may be tough to breathe and relax, but you can do it. Rest in peace confident that God is in control of all things, your storm included!*

THE ATTITUDE OF GRATITUDE

"One generation commends your works to another;
they tell of your mighty acts.
They speak of the glorious splendor of your majesty—
And I will meditate on your wonderful works."
~ PSALM 145:4–5 (NIV)

Daily Meditation: Psalm 145, Colossians 3:12–17

We women constantly need to judge between what is legitimately a need and what is simply a *want.* Often the lines are blurry, but there's no doubt about one thing that every woman absolutely, positively must have: gratitude.

To begin with, gratitude fuels our faith. When we choose to "meditate on your wonderful works" (because we know they truly are wonderful), our faith increases.

Gratitude also helps us believe our heavenly Father's promises because we remember what we are grateful for and, as a result, we become strong. What's more, gratitude makes us attractive. We smile, we praise others, and we laugh. Who doesn't want to be around someone like that?

And gratitude makes us wise, for we know whose we are, what we are, and where we are going. As I said, having an attitude of gratitude is a must!

> "Of all the attitudes, we can acquire, surely the
> attitude of gratitude is the most important
> and by far the most life changing."
> ~ ZIG ZIGLAR

BE FEARLESS: *expressing gratefulness makes me feel rich in every way. I think that is what God intended. Living with thankfulness and joy bring hope to my heart and brightens every step of my path!*

LET MY WORDS BRING LIFE

*"Do not be deceived: God cannot be
mocked. A man reaps what he sows."*
~ GALATIANS 6:7

Daily Meditation: Proverbs 15:1–4, Galatians 6

*Not everyone has an interest in planting flowers or a vegetable garden in the spring-*time, but every woman knows the power of the words we speak. Our words are seeds that will grow—they always produce a harvest grow—and will come back to haunt or bless us, exactly as it says: "Do not be deceived . . . a man reaps what he sows."

We've all heard the "sticks and stones will break my bones but words will never hurt me" jingle, but that does nothing to numb the pain of unkind words. I probably said that to myself a hundred times, but the pain still remained.

Our words are seeds, which mean they have the potential to bring life. Imagine blessing seeping into every crack and crevasse, every little part of your world! When the words we "plant" are good, healthy seeds, they bring life:

- for the speaker,
- for the listener,
- and for the watcher.

Since whatever we sow is going to come back to us, we'd be wise to plant good seeds everywhere!

> *"Don't judge each day by the harvest you reap*
> *but by the seeds that you plant."*
> ~ ROBERT LOUIS STEVENSON

———————

BE FEARLESS: *every plant begins as a seed. When we sow life-giving words in the soil of others' lives, we do not have to worry that what we've said will come back to haunt us. Instead we can look forward to what the Lord brings to fruition!*

I CHOOSE TO LEAP!

"Even though I walk through the darkest valley,
I will fear no evil, for you are with me;
your rod and your staff, they comfort me.
You prepare a table before me in the presence of my enemies."
~ Psalm 23:4–5a (NIV)

Daily Meditation: Matthew 14:28–32, John 10:7–18

Are you hanging on by a thread . . . feeling pushed to the edge of the cliff . . . hands aching from hanging on? Let go and leap!

Seriously, when are we going to take God at his word? I'm talking to myself here. How easily we forget that He is with us through thick and thin. Today I'm reminding myself that:

- I walk *through* "the darkest valley."
- I need not fear for He is "with me."
- He makes a table for me "in the presence of my enemies."

I don't stay in the darkest valley. I can live fearlessly each and every day knowing that He is going to bless me right smack dab in front of those who don't like me very much! Wow, that is my God at work on my behalf.

The choice is mine . . . and the choice is yours. Are we going to leap into His arms? That's right, today is all about trusting God. We're not talking about a tank of alligators or a lake of piranhas. This is about leaping into *His* arms. I say, "Get out of my way. I'm coming through!"

> *"Broken, I run to You*
> *For Your arms are open wide*
> *I am weary, but I know*
> *Your touch restores my life"*
> ~ KATHRYN SCOTT, "HUNGRY"

BE FEARLESS: *leaping is at once both scary and breathtakingly grand. Enjoy it! Choose to trust, to leap, and to be fully His! He is with you right now, this very second. He is your Father and you are his daughter. When you leap into His arms, you're in the safest place on earth!*

ABOUT THE AUTHOR

Julie Clinton M.Ad., M.B.A. is president of Extraordinary Women and host of Extraordinary Women conferences all across America. A woman of deep faith, she cares passionately about seeing women live out their dreams by finding their freedom in Christ. Julie and her husband, Dr. Tim Clinton, live in Virginia and are the parents of Zach and Megan, who is married to Ben Allison.

Dina Jones, M.A., is the Director of Professional and Public Relations for the American Association of Christian Counselors (AACC) and has served on the board of the Mid-Atlantic Career Counseling Association (MACCA). Dina Jones serves in the College of Arts and Sciences as an adjunct instructor for residential and online courses. Her areas of passion are career development and mental health for young parents. Dina and her husband are the parents of two precious young daughters and one son.

JOURNAL NOTES